ONLINE
MARKETING
FOR
PROFESSIONAL
SERVICES

"Online Marketing for Professional Services is a MUST READ for anyone involved with a professional services business. The Internet can be your most effective marketing tool but only with proper insight into your buyer and a comprehensive understanding of today's most effective online marketing tools. Hinge does it again with this powerful and effective guide."

MICHAEL FLEISCHNER, Founder of MarketingScoop.com

"If you want to be a major player in the A/E/C industry, read this book!"

RONALD D. WORTH, CAE, FSMPS, CPSM, Assoc AIA
CEO, Society for Marketing Professional Services

"This comprehensive, research-based book sheds light on how the online marketing revolution is affecting professional services firms. It provides readers with helpful considerations for strategy and implementation; the case studies and expert interviews present interesting perspectives throughout the book."

HOLLY BOLTON, FSMPS, CPSM
Director of Marketing, CE Solutions

"This is, without a doubt, the most important book on professional services marketing to have appeared for years. Not only does it comprehensively prove the case for the potential of online marketing for professional firms, it shows what to do to unlock that potential to drive profitability and growth. If you're responsible for running or marketing a professional service business you must read this book".

IAN BRODIE, Managing Director of the Rainmaker Academy.

"The Hinge Team has done it again! This book should be required reading for those in Professional Services. The book is chock full of amazing nuggets and best in class data delivered in a bright, fun, infotaining format. One is sure to feel much more educated about the current state of marketing in today's digital fast paced environment after reading this gem of a book!"

JENNIFER ABERNETHY, America's Social Business Stylist & CEO, The Sales Lounge

"I'm always skeptical of data from surveys. But Hinge does a good job at establishing causation through case studies and gives you a solid roadmap. This book is worth checking out."

MATT HANDAL, Author of *Proposal Development Secrets: Win More, Work Smarter, and Get Home on Time*

"Online Marketing for Professional Services is a fantastic guide to learning and understanding how to market your services online. If you are looking to increase the number of leads you generate online, you must read this book."

BRAD GEDDES, Founder of Certified Knowledge

"A must read for professional services firms who are making decisions about online marketing investments."

ERIC ENGE, Co-Author of *The Art of SEO*

"Honestly, this book is not just about developing an online marketing process that works for professional services companies...it's a total business roadmap. After the marketers in your organization read it, pass it to the C-suite. This stuff is that important for defining the future growth of your service company."

JOE PULIZZI, Founder of the Content Marketing Institute

Special discounts on bulk quantities of this book are available to corporations, professional associations and other organizations. For details contact *info@hingemarketing.com* or call **703.391.8870**.

Online Marketing for Professional Services, Copyright © 2012 by
Lee W. Frederiksen, Sean T. McVey, Sylvia Montgomery and Aaron E. Taylor

Published by Hinge Research Institute

12030 Sunrise Valley Drive, Suite 120
Reston, Virginia 20191

ISBN 978-0-9828819-3-4

Printed in the United States of America

Design by Hinge.

Visit our website at *www.hingemarketing.com*

ONLINE
MARKETING
FOR
PROFESSIONAL
SERVICES

Lee W. Frederiksen, Ph.D., Sean T. McVey,
Sylvia Montgomery, CPSM and Aaron E. Taylor

CONTENTS

ACKNOWLEDGEMENTS

A lot more effort goes into a book like this than meets the eye, and we would like to thank all the folks who contributed to this book in important ways but whose names don't appear on the cover: Candace Frederiksen, Brian Lemen, Kristin Claeys, Lee Eliav, Bethany Dawson, Shikha Savidas, Drew Ellis and everyone else at Hinge who made this possible. To Anne Scarlett and Matt Handal, thank you for reviewing the manuscript and offering invaluable suggestions.

We would also like to thank the 500 CEOs and senior executives who agreed to participate in the research study that sparked this book. In addition, we would like to extend our special thanks to the twenty online marketing experts who offered their keen insights and perspective to the study and this book.

Finally, we would like to thank the following organizations who helped us recruit study participants:

Society for Marketing Professional Services
www.smps.org

Association for Accounting Marketing
www.accountingmarketing.org

INTRODUCTION
How does your firm attract new clients?

C hances are, you rely on a handful of time-honored techniques such as client referrals, networking, tradeshow marketing, sponsorships, direct mail and maybe some print advertising or cold calls. They've served you well in the past. And you continue to rely on them year after year.

But we've got news for you. Your world is about to turn upside down.

You see, a revolution is underway. Online search, social media and email marketing are quickly and quietly overtaking traditional marketing tactics. Every year, more and more buyers turn to the Internet to help them find and select professional services providers. And this trend has dramatic implications for marketers like you. It means that the techniques that have worked in the past are likely to become less effective over time. And it means that if your firm is going to remain competitive over the next ten years, you need to embrace the online marketing tools that are redefining the way services are bought and sold.

In this book, we discuss online marketing's effect on both growth and profitability in the professional services. Using our research into 500 professional services firms, we explore the remarkable relationship between a firm's commitment to online marketing and high growth. We also dig deeper to uncover which techniques and tools high growth firms use most often. From this body of evidence, we've developed a roadmap that any firm — including yours — can follow to break into and master online marketing.

Happy marketing!

THE
REVOLUTION
IN
PROFESSIONAL
SERVICES
MARKETING

WELCOME TO THE REVOLUTION

Professional services marketing is undergoing profound change.

Whether or not you're aware of it, a revolution is afoot in the professional services marketplace. New, Internet-enabled technologies are challenging old assumptions about the way businesses buy professional services. While the personal referral — the longtime staple of professional services marketing — will always be important to business development, new forces are eating away at its dominance. Social media, content marketing and especially online search are turning marketing on its head.

Consider, for instance, how an executive today might approach a major service purchase:

Jacqueline: A Buyer's Story

This morning, Jacqueline — Vice President of Marketing at a regional web hosting service — has a problem. Sales are down for the second consecutive quarter. And just yesterday the executive team tasked her with slowing client attrition. The company's help desk collects a lot of data that might suggest an answer, but Jacqueline has no way to synthesize it into meaningful reports. Clearly, she needs software tools to help her understand the issue. But which one is best, and who's going to integrate it?

In the past, Jacqueline would have put out an RFP — a process that can take weeks or months. But this morning, she sits down at her laptop and launches Google. She tries a few keywords around the concepts of data mining and business intelligence. Within 15 minutes she has a list of seven promising-sounding companies and products. Over the next two hours, she looks at the companies' websites, watches demo videos and checks out online reviews. By noon, Jacqueline has narrowed down the list to three top options. She gives them a call, talks through the details and requests a proposal from each.

> It's clear to us that buyers' preferences are driving the changes in the professional services marketplace.

What used to take weeks is finished in a few hours. Even better, the nature of her search makes it easier to include geographically-diverse companies in the mix, so Jacqueline is able to choose among the best options in the country, not just the best in her region. And because she is able to evaluate each option quickly — including third-party reviews and what she reads on the company websites — she is able to weed out the weaker candidates.

Advantages of the New Way
Jacqueline is just one example of how the Internet is changing the way people buy services. Let's consider some of the most important ways that online marketing affects both buyers and sellers of services.

The Buyer's Perspective
It's clear to us that buyers' preferences are driving the changes in the professional services marketplace. Here are some

important benefits that are contributing to the industry's online marketing revolution:

Convenience — The traditional RFP is showing its age. For a fraction of the effort required to put together a structured request for proposal, a company can conduct an online search for qualified candidate firms.

Speed — As the example above demonstrates, online search can be fast and powerful. In a matter of minutes, a person can pull together a bevy of qualified options.

Greater Variety — The Internet provides access to a much broader spectrum of service providers than a typical RFP process can reach.

More Geographic Diversity — With variety comes exposure to every corner of the country and the globe. As a result, buyers are becoming more comfortable considering far-flung service providers.

Familiar Process — Today's buyers are used to searching for goods and services online in their personal lives. So they are naturally inclined to bring the power and convenience of online shopping into their professional lives. And many of these individuals have used social media tools in their private lives, so they are comfortable asking for referrals online or conducting their own impromptu research.

DAVID MEERMAN SCOTT
Author, *The New Rules of Marketing and PR*

"Publishing thought leadership content is a way to show potential customers that you have the ability to solve their problems."

3

The Marketer's Perspective

Many firms find the transition from traditional to online marketing painful at first. But once they've made the commitment, marketers discover that online marketing offers many advantages they didn't have before.

Flexible — There are legions of online marketing tools out there, so a marketer has a lot of options at her disposal. Many of these tools let you test different approaches. And if a tool doesn't work out, it's usually easy to move on to something else.

Measurable — Many online tools make it easy to track your progress. Savvy marketers will use this information to optimize their approach and make more money.

Adjustable — Making tactical or strategic changes on the fly is instantaneous and relatively easy.

Less Expensive — Compared to the expense of traditional marketing (such as printing, postage and travel expenses), online marketing is relatively cheap. On the other hand, the more you invest in it, the greater your potential return.

> Online tools make it easy to track your progress.

Largely Automated — Many online tools work tirelessly in the background — 24/7/365. Some can be connected to CRMs, so that leads and other data are collected (and, if desired, responded to) automatically.

Geographic Reach — Many local or regional firms are finding it easier to engage a national and global audience. Online tools make it relatively easy to target businesses anywhere.

More Effective — As you will see later in this book, online marketing is associated with some of the fastest-growing professional services firms. This relationship is no accident.

An Emerging New Path

Many firms are still unaware that a change is underway. As online marketing accelerates and old techniques begin to falter, firms that ignore these trends will be vulnerable. The chapters that follow will help you see more clearly and avoid losing touch with change.

Online tools make it relatively easy to target businesses anywhere.

As in any revolution, it can be difficult to see your way through the smoke. But a new path is emerging. Before you take your first steps, however, you need to understand the place where much of this change is happening: the buyer's brain.

Key Takeaways

- The Internet is changing the way professional services are bought and sold.

- Online marketing will help your firm adapt to the the new marketplace.

- The Internet is a faster, more convenient and more powerful way to shop for services.

- Online marketing offers more flexibility, control and geographic reach than traditional marketing methods.

- Firms that don't adopt online marketing are at risk.

CASE STUDY
Kinaxis: A Well-Oiled Online Marketing Program

Imagine you are VP of Marketing Communications at a major supply chain management software company. You know online marketing has a place, but you really don't know where to focus. Do you hire a social media guru? Do you invest in video? SEO? A blog? The possibilities are endless... but your budget isn't. How do you spend?

Kirsten Watson from Kinaxis was in this very situation. And after a long digital journey, she finds herself today leading one of the most successful online marketing teams in the technology industry. With about 40% of their leads coming from the web, Kinaxis has found a formula for success.

Make Friends with the Search Engines
"We found religion in SEO," said Kirsten. "It's a part of everything we do, every content piece, every campaign." They carefully research keyword opportunities, and implement those keywords into their website.

Create a Community by Creating Content
A blog not only demonstrates thought leadership, but also attracts high-quality inbound links and increases the number of web pages indexed in search engines. "We blogged for about a year," said Kirsten, "but nobody was listening at first. You have to have

patience, and visibility will come. After a while the traffic became consistent and highly beneficial."

Once You're in the Groove, Start to Get Social
The team was a bit skeptical of social media at first. But research firm Forrester showed them how Kinaxis' audience uses social platforms, how they comment and where they hang out.
This data served as the basis for a social media strategy that ultimately boosted the company's online visibility.

Time to Go Above and Beyond
Today, Kinaxis is taking their marketing to a new level. Their Supply Chain Expert Community is a collection of videos, forums, and documents related to supply chain management. *Late Late Supply Chain Show* and *Suitemates* are examples of how they create buzz and pull in relevant traffic. "We recognize that we need to take chances to get noticed," said Kirsten. "We're not afraid of sticking out our neck a little so we can be heard."

Bringing It All Together
Kinaxis' monthly process goes something like this:
1. Choose a promising keyword phrase
2. Write an article or white paper using that phrase
3. Break the paper into blog posts and repurpose the content
4. Interview the author on video and post it on the website
5. Create a podcast
6. Host a webinar
7. Promote the content through social media and email communication

Kinaxis devotes five people to online marketing, including two full-time content creators, one full-time events manager, a social media manager and Kristen. Eighteen other staff members also contribute content, including top executives.

The company's highest-quality leads come from search engine traffic, so the investment makes a lot of sense.

★ INSIDE THE BUYER'S ★ BRAIN

We are researching and purchasing everything
else online. Why not professional services?

To understand the factors driving the revolution in professional services marketing, you need to understand what's happening between the ears of prospective buyers.

At some point, an issue arises in their company that requires expert attention. What do they do?

If it's an issue they don't completely understand, they'll likely turn to their computers (or tablets or smartphones) and Google it. In most cases, searchers will find a wide range of information that explains the issue. Often, the best information they find online is written by experts at firms that specialize in a related service.

Once educated enough to understand what kind of help they need, buyers will often turn again to a search engine (usually Google) to research firms that can help them solve their problem. Sometimes, that includes the firm that just educated them on the issue. They may also ask other professionals for a referral or post a question in an online forum.

Once they've compiled a list of promising service providers, buyers will check out these firms' websites, read LinkedIn profiles of key team members and look into references.

Anyone who entered the workforce in the last decade grew up with digital devices.

If all of this sounds familiar, it should come as no surprise. The process of finding information and relevant business expertise online is so easy, even senior executives get into the act. And it's an increasingly common scenario being played out in organizations around the world. Why is this the case? What does it mean for your firm?

The March of Technology

Today, we do things differently because we can. Over the last couple of decades computing power has become ubiquitous. The cost of global communication has plummeted. And the amount of information instantly available to anyone with an Internet connection is astonishing.

Technology has even transformed social functions such as professional networking and communicating with friends. Witness the rise of social media. If you Skype with your grandkids, why not your clients?

But technology is only the start. Other forces are at work.

Digital Demographics

Anyone who entered the workforce in the last decade grew up with digital devices. Just as an earlier generation grew up with telephones, today's young workers are completely comfortable with computers and mobile devices — and even take them for granted. They use these devices to communicate with friends and colleagues, check out movies and restaurants, buy books and music, and meet new people, maybe even a spouse. With technology so ingrained in our lives, why not use it to find or evaluate a new professional services provider? It's natural!

The Time Pressured Executive

Do more with less. Work smarter, work faster. Today's executives are under more pressure to accomplish more, faster than ever before. In a highly competitive global environment, there is little inclination to fool with time-consuming approaches to solving problems.

"I want the solution now. Who can solve my problem with minimal input from me or my team? We need a solution to our challenge that gives us confidence. Where can I find that firm with the minimum of hassle and time commitment?"

I want the solution now.

Online marketing offers an easy answer to this question.

Expectations of Free Education

When you go online you expect to find a wealth of educational material. The basics of almost any topic are literally at your fingertips. You may have to register — provide your name and email address, for instance — to access some resources, but that's a small price to pay for valuable information, especially if it can help your business. And certain in-depth materials such as books or proprietary research may require payment. But by and large, in the world of the Internet you expect to learn for free.

KRISTINA HALVERSON
Author, *Content Stratgegy for the Web*

"Executives are reading white papers less these days because they become irrelevant quickly. They will read blog posts and tweets. What content formats you choose to produce depends on who you are trying to reach and how they consume information."

This experience has direct implications for your professional services firm. Do you want to be the place prospects come to learn about emerging issues? Or do you want them to go somewhere else? How much of your expertise do you give away? And what do you sell?

There was a time when the answers to these questions were fairly easy. If you wanted to tap into a firm's expertise, you needed to hire them. That's not so clear anymore. Today, hiding all your expertise behind a wall can put you at a decided disadvantage in the competition for new clients.

If a competitor of yours is forthcoming and generous about educating potential clients and you are opaque, where do you think that potential client will turn when they need to hire expertise?

Expectations of Transparency

Who works at your firm? What are they like to work with? Who are your clients? How do you approach certain problems? In the past, many firms would have considered these questions sensitive and been loath to share.

But these days, many prospective clients see them as legitimate areas of inquiry. Prospects should be able to go online and learn all about your firm, philosophy and approach. If buyers can't easily access this kind of information, they are likely to pass you over for a firm that has nothing to hide.

Today's Internet-savvy buyers also expect to learn about a firm's strengths and weaknesses. After all, they can go online and find reviews of restaurants, physicians, books and new cars. Why not accounting firms or IT consultants? What are you trying to hide?

Geography is becoming less of a barrier to doing business.

A Global Marketplace

All of these trends tend to move us in a clear direction. Competition for professional services is expanding geographically — beyond a shallow pool of local providers. It's becoming easier and easier to find specific services anywhere in the country or world.

While there is no substitute for face-to-face interaction, businesses are becoming comfortable conducting business remotely. From services such as GoToMeeting, WebEx and Skype to the routine use of email and conference calls, geography is becoming less of a barrier to doing business.

Many professional services firms are already working with clients outside their local markets and developing specialized services that are more "exportable." Whether or not your firm has aspirations to expand geographically, you have competitors that do and potential clients who are comfortable trading local access for greater expertise.

The Specialist's Advantage

All of these trends point toward something we call the specialist's advantage. If a business is looking for a firm to solve a specific problem, it is more likely, given the choice, to select a firm that specializes in solving similar problems for clients like them — often with little regard for physical location. Thanks to the Internet, specialists are getting easier and easier to find and evaluate.

Generalists, even if they are local and have a good relationship with a potential client, may have difficulty competing against specialized firms. This inherent advantage may be one of the keys behind our finding that firms with clearly defined target clients and specialties tend to grow much faster and experience a higher level of profitability.[1]

Specialists are getting easier and easier to find and evaluate.

---

1 *Spiraling Up: How to Create a High Growth, High Value Professional Services Firm* (2010). Download a free copy at *www.hingemarketing.com/spiralingup*

A Compelling Case for Online Marketing

With all of these factors favoring online marketing, one might expect to see a decided advantage for professional services firms that embrace it. As it turns out, that is exactly what we found.

Key Takeaways

- Technology, demographics and time pressure are driving buyers of professional services to look online for education and solutions.

- They expect to find a free education and world-class expertise.

- Specialists who are very visible and transparent about their capabilities have a competitive advantage.

- Geography is becoming less of a factor in buying decisions.

CASE STUDY

Mazuma: Selling Accounting Services to the iPhone Generation

Mazuma, a UK-based accounting services company, generates approximately 80% of its business online. While most professional services firms are still trying to figure out how to update their websites, Mazuma is finding new ways to connect with youthful prospects — and perhaps paving the way for the rest of the accounting industry.

How does one go about selling accounting services to younger folks? It's certainly not through handshakes and sales calls. Lucy Cohen, cofounder of Mazuma, shared some key concepts that are driving their success.

If you want to connect with the mobile generation, you need to look good on a mobile phone.

Approximately 38% of Mazuma's website traffic comes through mobile platforms, such as smartphones and tablets. Mobile traffic has significantly increased worldwide within the past year, and the percentage of visitors using mobile will only continue to climb.

Lucy and her team quickly realized that creating a mobile-friendly website was a top priority. A better website experience for potential clients equates to more trust, more engagement and more conversions of visitors into sales.

Figure out how younger prospects want to receive information... then give them what they want.

Most young professionals don't read direct mail and don't have the patience for traditional advertising. Yet 70% of Mazuma's clients are under the age of 40. The Mazuma team has figured out how to engage and connect with the younger crowd.

The firm leverages e-newsletters and other email marketing tools to establish that connection. Every client receives 36 "Mazuma touches" per year, which include a mix of email offers and less formal check-ins from company reps. Because Mazuma's newsletter open rate is more than double the industry average, it's safe to say their approach is on point.

Young people don't read; they watch. Embrace video.

Have you noticed that written text on websites is starting to decrease? For many people, video is a more efficient way to learn about a product or service. Lucy and the Mazuma team do a great job of meeting the video demand, using short clips on their website to describe their service and generate credibility.

Their primary company video pieces together testimonial interviews, depicting satisfied clients who tout the efficiency and ease of Mazuma's unorthodox approach. Professionally produced video adds personal credibility to a brand that's not based on personal relationships. Mazuma's two-minute production is more effective at engaging its target audience than many traditional accounting firm websites.

★ TWO PATHS TO TRUST ★

Is there a better way to build trust?

Trust may be the most fundamental tenet of professional services marketing. How can you expect a potential client to retain you if they don't trust you? You can't.

Conversely, the pinnacle of professional services marketing is achieving the status of "trusted advisor" — that magical point in a relationship when your client instinctively turns to you for advice on problems that lie — even remotely — in your realm of expertise.

How can you achieve this lofty status?

Obviously, you have to prove yourself trustworthy. But before that can happen, you first have to get the clients. Historically, that's started with developing a relationship.

Golfing for Clients

When you talk about a relationship, most folks think face-to-face interaction. And for most of human history that's how relationships have been developed.

In the world of professional services, business development has translated into countless networking events, memberships on the boards of non-profits, industry trade association conferences and, of course, golf outings. Familiarity comes first. From there a cordial personal relationship develops along with exposure to your professional expertise. This combination leads to trust.

MARI SMITH
Author, *The New Relationship Marketing*

"It's highly important to both create unique content and promote content from others. I believe it's vital to add your own opinion into the mix if you want to position yourself as an authority."

Only then does the business relationship develop.

This traditional model looks something like this:

Meet → Relationship → Expertise → Trust → Client

This tried-and-true formula has worked for many years. And it still works today. But there are a few problems with this approach.

First, it's slow and labor intensive. Developing personal relationships takes time. Board meetings, conferences, networking receptions and other face-to-face techniques require significant investments of time from senior people. Consequently, these activities are very expensive, and there is a limit to how much of it any one person can do.

Second, face-to-face client development can be hit and miss. You may be at the right networking event, but don't happen to run into the one person who needs your service. Business development can seem accidental and unpredictable.

Finally, it tends to be focused locally. Sure, there are national and international conferences, but most networking has a decidedly local orientation.

Without much fanfare, a robust alternative to the traditional approach to developing professional services business has evolved. Think of it as an online path to trust.

Surfing for Clients

This online path to trust has arisen from the way people use the Internet to educate themselves about business issues. It works something like this:

Developing personal relationships takes time.

A business is experiencing a new challenge that internal resources alone can't overcome. Perhaps it's a new regulation or a need to improve productivity in the organization. To gain some perspective on the issue, an executive at the company opens her laptop, fires up Google and types in some search terms.

As she skims the results, her eye is caught by an overview that explains the issue in plain language and lays out alternative approaches. The more this executive investigates, the more she concludes the company needs to retain a consultant to help it tackle the issue.

Next, she begins to compile a list of potential experts. She is drawn immediately to the person who wrote the overview article. The author clearly knew his stuff and seemed to have a good grasp of the issues involved. She then searches for consultants who specialize in the problem facing her company.

Will it help you grow faster or be more profitable?

The executive does much of this searching in Google, but she also inquires on an online forum and emails some of her industry contacts.

The executive was pleasantly surprised to see a familiar name appear a couple of times in the responses — the author of the first online article she read on the subject. Clearly this was a trustworthy source who understood her challenges. She put this expert at the top of her list to contact.

In this scenario, and many real-life ones, the online model goes something like this:

Issue → Education → Expert → Trust → Client

This model is well suited to the online world where so many of us operate every day. It offers several advantages:

• Very easily leveraged

• Not tied to geography or time zone

• Can be less expensive to implement

• Works 24 hours a day, every day

It also has limitations. Online marketing does not offer face-to-face interactions and it relies on your ability to be "found" for the right issues. In many ways, it's almost the antithesis of the traditional model.

How Well Does Online Marketing Work?

The obvious question is "How well does it work?" Is online marketing a viable alternative for your professional services firm? Will it help you grow faster or be more profitable?

Well, there seems to be an unending flow of opinion around topics such as social media, SEO, and other online marketing tools. Most of these opinions stream from advocates with an ax to grind. But there's surprisingly little hard evidence out there to make a truly informed decision.

But that is about to change.

Key Takeaways

- Building trust is a cornerstone of professional services marketing.

- Traditionally, trust has been established by building relationships through repeated face-to-face interaction.

- An alternative path to building trust involves sharing useful expertise online.

- The key question is around the cost effectiveness of this new online model.

THE
RESULTS
ARE IN

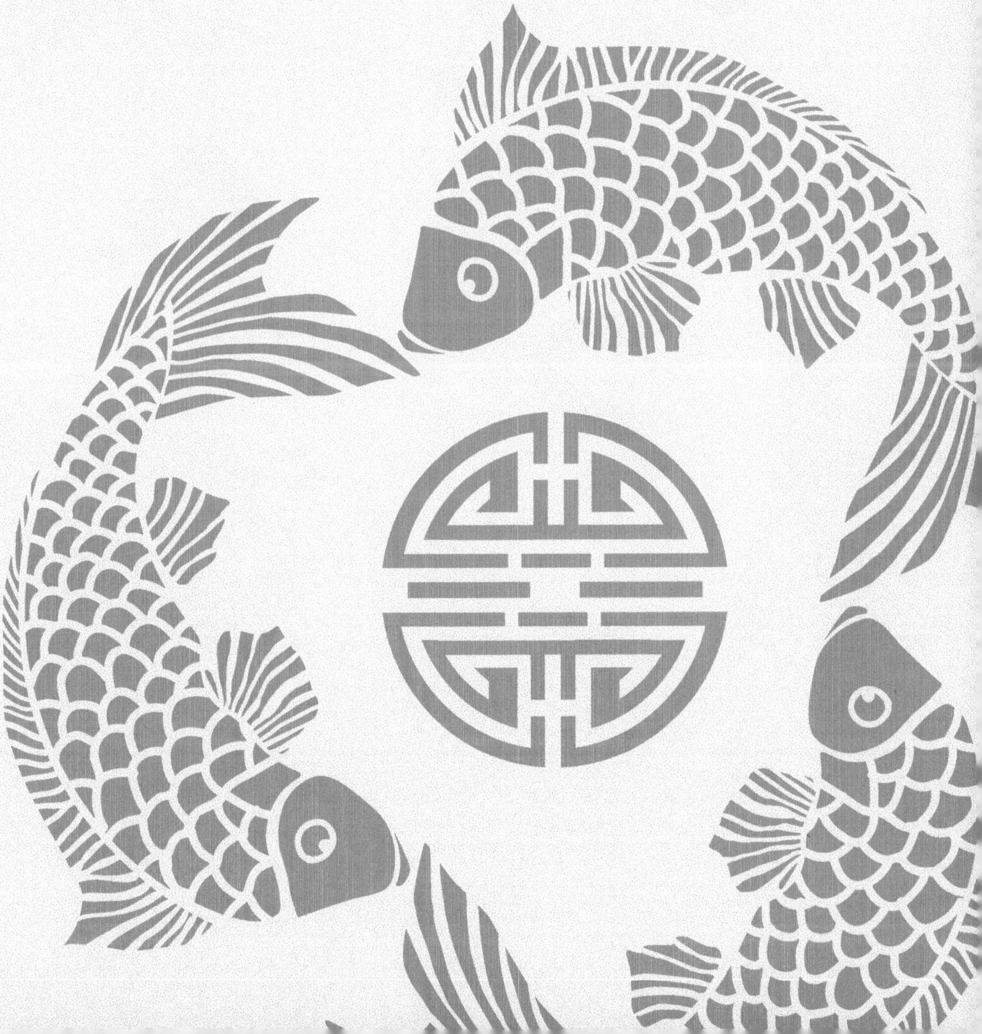

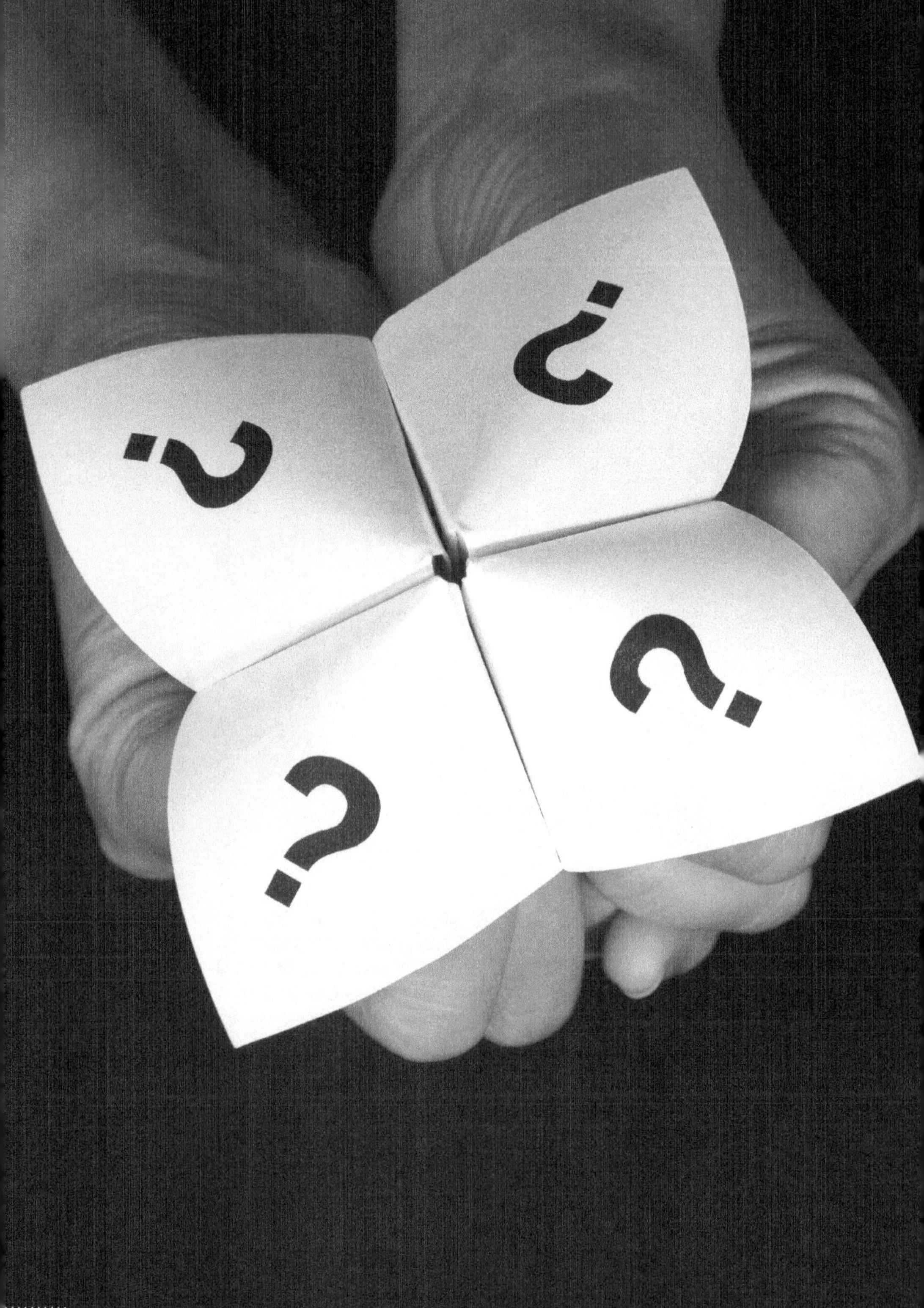

UNRAVELING THE ONLINE MARKETING MYSTERY

Discovering what really works
in the digital world.

There is no shortage of opinions about online marketing. The marketing world produces a steady supply of self-proclaimed experts, each advocating their own particular approach.

This hullabaloo is particularly noticeable in the realm of social media. It's easy to get sucked into the whirlpool of excitement and sweeping claims. The reality is often quite different. Many firms jump into social media with the best of intentions only to find that nothing seems to be happening. No leads, no new business. So they lose interest or give up completely in the belief that online marketing doesn't work for professional services.

Even firms deeply committed to a digital future can be unsure where to begin and how to proceed. That alone might have been reason enough for us to conduct a study on professional services online marketing. But we had another, even more compelling reason.

There is no shortage of opinions about online marketing.

The High Growth Imperative

At our firm, Hinge, we have a strong commitment to understanding the high growth, high value professional services firm.[2] This fixation compelled us to conduct a series of studies to determine exactly what these firms do differently from their average growth competitors.

High growth firms are much more likely to focus on their websites than their average growth peers.

The results of this effort have been documented in our recent book, *Spiraling Up: How to Create a High Growth, High Value Professional Services Firm*, where we found that high growth firms grow up to 9X faster and are 50% more profitable while still spending slightly less than average on business development. While we uncovered many important strategies and marketing approaches used by high growth firms, one thing stood out to us.

High growth firms are much more likely to focus on their websites than their average growth peers. This was a clue that merited further investigation.

Two Big Questions

In thinking about the design of the study, we realized there were two important questions we wanted to answer.

1. Does online marketing make business sense for professional services firms? Can it help them grow faster or be more profitable? Is there really a return on the investment?

2. If it does make business sense, what is the right way to do it? What techniques and approaches really work in the professional services context? Just because an approach works for a consumer product doesn't mean it translates to a professional service.

---

2 We define a high growth firm as one that demonstrates a minimum growth rate of 20% over each of the past two consecutive years.

A Bold Approach

These questions were not going to be easy to answer. As we looked around we weren't able to find any research that had attempted to tie online marketing directly to business performance. Sure, a lot of online marketing advocates had speculated that it might, but it seemed that no one had actually done the work to find the real answer.

We decided that the best approach was to relate an objective indicator of online marketing performance to objective measures of financial performance, such as firm growth and profitability. The indicator we chose was the percentage of new business leads generated online.

We also realized that to establish a meaningful relationship we would have to look across a large number of firms from a broad cross section of professional services industries. We chose to investigate 500 firms from across the United States.

JASON BURBY
Author, *Actionable Web Analytics*

"Judging success is going to vary from company to company. You must agree upon goals and what success means across the organization. Don't focus on all of the data. Step back and ask yourselves what really matters to the firm. That could be the number of leads, the number of recruits or other important data points."

The resulting sample included firms with an average of 319 employees and almost $54 million in revenue.

A total of **{500}** professional services **firms** completed the survey.

319 average employees

Average firm size:
$53,929,835 annual revenue

Our sample included five primary industry groups shown in Fig. 1.

Fig. 1. Sample Composition by Industry Group

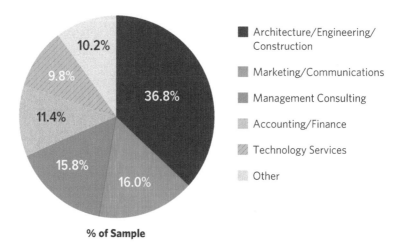

% of Sample

The firms in the sample do various levels of government contracting.

Fig. 2. Government Contracting Mix

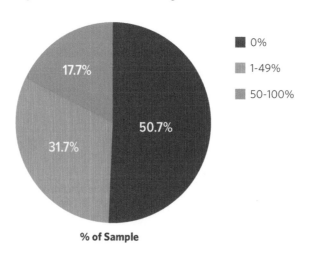

% of Sample

The respondents themselves were overwhelmingly senior executives in their firms.

Fig. 3. Position in Firm

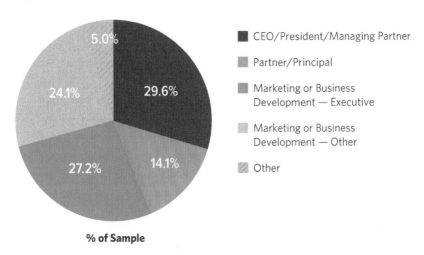

- CEO/President/Managing Partner
- Partner/Principal
- Marketing or Business Development — Executive
- Marketing or Business Development — Other
- Other

% of Sample

Clearing Away Confusion

If we were able to establish a relationship between firm performance and online marketing, we would need to answer these questions: which techniques achieve the best results? And how should firms organize their efforts?

We took two approaches to answer these questions. First we looked to the high growth firms. Do high growth firms use specific techniques differently than average growth firms, and how effective are these techniques in helping them reach their objectives?

First we looked to the high growth firms.

Second, we recruited a panel of 20 top online marketing experts to help us calibrate the potential effectiveness of each of the techniques for professional services firms. We've listed these experts in the Appendix and you will encounter some of their insights throughout the book. We reasoned that top experts who helped develop and refine these techniques would have the best understanding of their optimal use.

Now all that remained was the voice of the data.

Key Takeaways

- While there are many opinions about online marketing, empirical facts are few.

- To investigate the impact of online marketing, we studied 500 professional services firms.

- We also assembled a panel of 20 top online marketing experts.

- We chose to focus on what high growth firms do differently from their peers.

- We also investigated the impact of individual online marketing tools.

CASE STUDY
PrimePay and Social Media: 7 Game Changing Tips

PrimePay, a leading payroll, tax, HR, insurance and benefit services company, is using social media to great affect. Nancy Mullin, Manager of Marketing and Interactive Services, offers these 7 tips:

1. *Determine Your Conversion Actions* – PrimePay tracks specific goals on its site. For instance, they want visitors to fill out their contact form (their primary call to action) and download credibility-building documents, such as their Employee Handbook (a secondary call to action). Having trackable goals is an important step to building a lead-generating website.

2. *Eliminate Friction* – PrimePay's old website had one major problem: it did not make it easy for people to contact the company. The new site, however, makes it incredibly easy to contact the firm or take a conversion action. Simplified web forms and clear calls to action have led to an influx of leads.

3. *Meet Your New Best Friend: The CRM* – The team benefits greatly from using a Customer Relationship Management (CRM) tool called HubSpot. This type of software allows you to create new web forms and offers, track leads by source and segment your list of prospects for easy email marketing. This tool has dramatically increased PrimePay's efficiency.

4. *Pluck Low Hanging Fruit* – When it comes to ranking in search engines, PrimePay's strategy is to find keyword opportunities that haven't yet been saturated. Rather than target high-volume, highly competitive phrases, they target many more-attainable keyword phrases. The traffic they receive from these highly targeted "long-tail" keywords adds up.

5. *Declare Yourself the Authority, Then Back It Up* – In the world of professional services, trust is everything. PrimePay not only declared themselves a thought leader, but they supported the claim by stepping up their effort to publish educational content for business owners, payroll professionals, accountants and brokers. This long-term strategy has led to a brand that prospects can trust.

6. *Blog on Topics that Generate Leads* – When producing educational content, PrimePay always has a specific target demographic in mind. They write posts that speak the language of their target readers and attract qualified leads. These posts are intended to be discovered by HR professionals who — either now or in the future — may need assistance.

7. *Stick. It. Out.* – "It's tough in the beginning," explained Nancy. "You're writing all of these posts, you don't have many subscribers and you start to think... is this worth it? We stuck it out, and it paid off." You can't climb this mountain overnight. PrimePay made it through the hard times and now they are reaping the rewards.

ONLINE MARKETING
★ DRIVES GROWTH AND ★
PROFITABILITY

There really is a better way.

E very marketer who has spent a half a day at a fruitless networking event or waited for a referral that never materialized has probably had the same fantasy. If only there were a way to generate qualified leads that didn't require precious hours away from billable work — one that was predictable and scalable.

Well, that's precisely the allure of online lead generation.

77%
of professional services firms generate new business leads online.

Prevalence of Online Lead Generation
In our study, we found that over 77% of professional services firms generate new business leads online. Almost half of the firms, about 48%, get less than 1 in 5 of their leads that way (see Fig. 4, next page).

But what is the upside potential for digital lead generation? As the accompanying figure shows, almost 15% of firms are getting at least 40% of new business leads from online marketing.

Fig. 4. Online Lead Generation

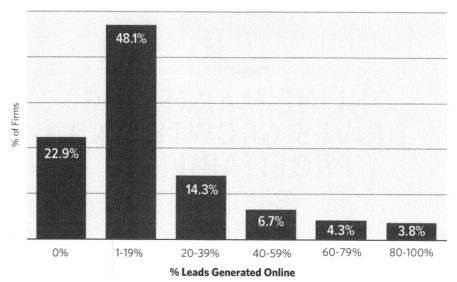

Online Lead Generation by Industry

So how do the various professional services industry groups fare? Clearly, not all industry groups are performing at the same level (see Fig. 5). While A/E/C firms average just over 8% of leads from online sources, marketing and communications firms are above 30%. All other industries studied range between 10 and 20%.

Fig. 5. Online Lead Generation by Industry

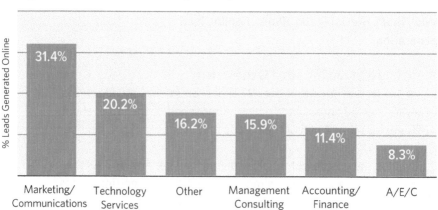

How do government contractors fare? As Fig. 6 shows, the group of firms with the highest proportion of government contracts has the lowest level of online lead generation. Of course, government contractors rely less on traditional business development activities than other professional services. Much (and in some cases, most) of their business comes through a structured RFP process rather than personal relationships and trust.

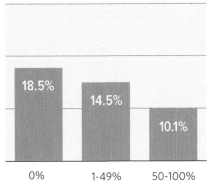

Fig. 6. Lead Generation and Government Contracting

% Leads Generated Online

18.5%   14.5%   10.1%

0%   1-49%   50-100%

% Revenue from Government Contracting

While our study didn't investigate the cause of this relationship, one possible factor is that online lead generation in the A/E/C industry. Historically, firms within A/E/C tend to do a fair amount of government business.

Keep in mind, though, that firms from all industry segments are successfully generating leads online. Only some industries are doing it more consistently. But what is the impact on their financial performance?

Firms from all industry segments are successfully generating leads online.

Lead Generation and Firm Growth

Is online lead generation associated with faster firm growth?
Fig. 7 provides a clear answer.

Fig. 7. Firm Growth and Online Lead Generation

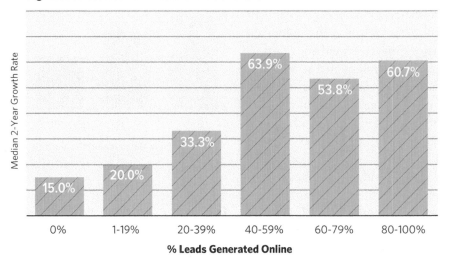

As the proportion of leads generated online increases so does
the rate of growth of the firm (this applies across all industry
groups). This relationship holds until 40% or more of leads
come from digital sources. Above that, growth rate levels off.

Firms that aren't generating any leads online average 15%
median growth over the two-year study period.

Contrast that growth rate to the firms that generated at least
40% of their new business leads online. Their growth over
the same two-year time period was approximately 4 times
that amount.

So unless you believe that faster growth causes greater
online lead generation (not so likely), you are left with a clear
conclusion. Online lead generation drives faster firm growth.

If you can somehow attract qualified leads online (more on this later), while continuing your normal networking and referral activity, you might reasonably expect faster growth. But what about firm profitability? Does online lead generation pay off financially?

Lead Generation and Firm Profitability

Here again, the results tell a clear story. Fig. 8 shows firm profitability as a percentage of revenue for each of the different levels of online lead generation.

Online lead generation drives faster firm growth.

Fig. 8. Profitability and Online Lead Generation

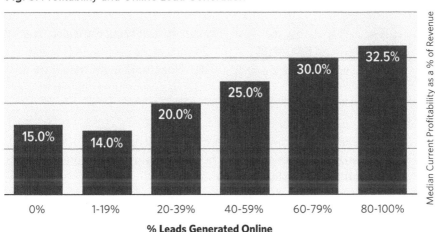

Up to 20%, online lead generation profits remain level. Above that point we see a clear trend. As online lead generation rises so does profitability. A firm generating 60% or more of leads digitally is likely to be twice as profitable as one generating less than 20% of new business online.

This outcome makes perfect sense, as online lead generation can be less expensive than traditional approaches. In fact, one recent study cites a 62% cost advantage.[3]

---

3 Source: Hubspot, *The 2012 State of Inbound Marketing*

High Growth Firms and Online Lead Generation

If this relationship holds true, we would expect to find the high growth firms we studied getting a relatively large proportion of their leads online, and they would tend to be more profitable than their average growth peers. Indeed, that's exactly what we found.

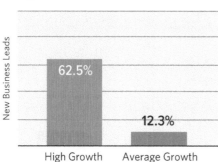

Fig. 9. Online Leads

High growth firms were much more likely to generate leads online (see Fig. 9). While average firms generated 12% of leads online, high growth firms generated over 62% of new business leads digitally.

High growth firms were also over 2 times more profitable (see Fig. 10). Not surprisingly, their growth rate was many times higher as well (see Fig. 11).

Clearly, high growth firms are taking full advantage of digital marketing to generate new business. But is there more to digital marketing than lead generation?

That's where we go next.

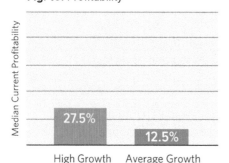

Fig. 10. Profitability

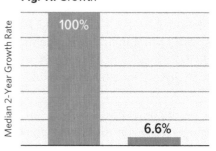

Fig. 11. Growth

Key Takeaways

- About 77% of professional services firms generate new business leads online.

- Lead generation varies by industry.

- Firms that generate 40% or more of their leads online grow 4 times faster.

- As online lead generation rises, so does profitability.

- High growth firms generate more leads online.

CHAPTER 6

★ BEYOND LEAD ★
GENERATION

Recruiting and brand building
in the digital world.

U p to this point, our focus has been on new business development
and how online marketing drives faster growth and greater
profitability. But new clients are of limited value if you don't have
quality staff to serve them.

In most professional services industries, this is no small problem. In the
research behind our previous book, *Spiraling Up*, we found that recruiting
quality people is often a top concern of managing partners and CEOs.
Chances are, you share this concern. No people, no services rendered.

And what about your firm's brand? How do you
shape your reputation and increase visibility in
an online world? All good questions. We'll take
a look at both in this chapter.

New clients
are of limited
value if you
don't have
quality staff to
serve them.

55%

of firms get new hires online.

Online Recruiting

Over half of the professional services firms we studied recruit new employees online (see Fig. 12). 55% of firms get new hires online. While 45% of firms don't attract any new people in this way, a surprising number rely on it quite heavily. About one in four firms generate 40% or more of their new hires online.

How does online recruiting relate to the financial performance of professional services firms? When we looked at all the firms in our study, we found no evident relationship between the percent of online hires and either growth or profitability.

Fig. 12. Online Recruiting

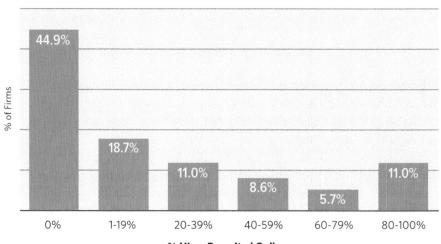

% of Firms

44.9%

18.7%

11.0%

8.6%

5.7%

11.0%

0%   1-19%   20-39%   40-59%   60-79%   80-100%

% Hires Recruited Online

But when we compared high growth firms to average firms we noticed an interesting correlation (see Fig. 13). High growth firms get over twice as many new hires online.

Online Recruiting by Industry

The percent of new hires recruited online varies by industry (see Fig. 14). Technology services lead the way with over 27% of hires coming from online marketing. Accounting/ Finance recruits about half that many.

Firms that do a great deal of government contracting are also much more likely to rely on online recruiting (see Fig. 15 on the next page). While we found that they lag in online lead generation, government contractors are leaders in online recruiting. Similarly, A/E/C firms generate relatively few leads online but do much better in online recruiting.

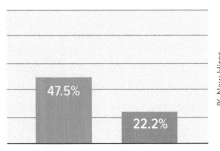

Fig. 13. Online Hires in High Growth vs. Average Growth Firms

% New Hires

47.5%

22.2%

High Growth   Average Growth

Fig. 14. Online Recruiting by Industry

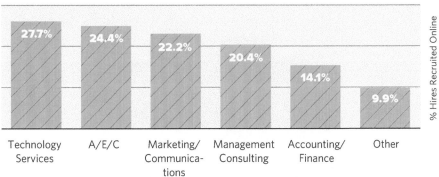

% Hires Recruited Online

27.7%   24.4%   22.2%   20.4%   14.1%   9.9%

Technology Services | A/E/C | Marketing/ Communications | Management Consulting | Accounting/ Finance | Other

Prisoners of Our Industry?

So if you are in an industry that generates few leads online or lags in online recruiting, is your firm doomed to languish in the doldrums? Is online marketing worth the effort?

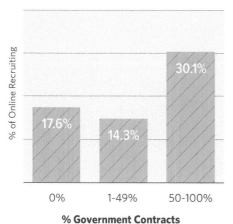

Fig. 15. Online Recruiting and Government Contracting

% of Online Recruiting

17.6%
14.3%
30.1%

0%   1-49%   50-100%

% Government Contracts

Clearly, there are important differences between industries that must be taken into account. These differences will inevitably influence some of the choices that you make. But there is a hidden danger here.

It's easy to fall into a trap and convince yourself that your industry is unique: Your clients don't go online to learn about business issues. They don't read your firm's website or care about what people say about you in social media. And potential employees in your industry don't find jobs online.

This is a dangerous belief system.

In each of the industries we studied — even the stragglers—
there were many firms that leverage online marketing.

A Competitive Disadvantage

If you are sitting on the sidelines contemplating
whether online marketing makes sense for your
firm, you should be aware that many of your
competitors are not so complacent. Consider
some of these facts.

Fully 66% of firms plan to increase their online
marketing budget this year. The average
increase is 56%. And this is not a new trend.
Over 46% of the firms we studied had already redesigned their
website within the past 12 months.

Fully 66% of
firms plan to
increase their
online marketing
budget this
year.

The push to embrace online marketing is already well on its way.
Firms that do not embrace the trend will likely be operating at a
competitive disadvantage sooner than later.

Your Brand Online

So far, we've focused mostly on how online marketing drives
quantitative outcomes such as new business leads and new
hires. There is another set of online marketing goals that is not
as easily quantified. Think of them as brand building.

When we consider brand building for the professional services,
we see two primary tasks. The first is to improve or shape a
firm's reputation. The second is to increase the visibility of that
reputation within a firm's target audience.

While not as easy to measure as lead generation or recruiting,
brand building is very important. Most executives understand
the importance of their firm's reputation and visibility within
the marketplace. What they may not fully appreciate is the huge
role that their online presence plays in building it.

Branding Impacts
Consider these three scenarios.

1. A job candidate who is a perfect fit with your firm graduates from a college in your region. While conducting a job search he runs across your firm and visits your website. He is impressed with what he sees so he applies and is hired. He also visited three of your direct competitors and never applied to any of them because they didn't "feel right."

2. A great potential client goes to several LinkedIn groups to ask for referrals for a project that is right up your alley. Your firm is never recommended by anyone in the groups.

3. One of your best clients refers a friend to your firm. The friend visits your website and concludes your firm is just "not in her league," so she never contacts you.

Your online brand has a direct impact on your business, whether you are aware of it or not.

Each of these scenarios is real. And they illustrate a key point: your online brand has a direct impact on your business, whether you are aware of it or not.

Online Branding
Think about online branding this way: Your firm's reputation and visibility exist in the minds of your target audience, referral sources, clients, and competitors. Historically, these impressions grew out of direct experience with your firm, as well as what they read or heard about you. That hasn't changed.

What *has* changed is that prospective buyers and employees increasingly are seeing, reading and hearing things online. From a webinar they attend to an eBook they read to an offhand comment made in a social media group, critical audiences are learning about people and firms on the Internet. Reputations are being made just like they have always been. Only now, it's happening online.

Key Takeaways

- 55% of firms get at least some new hires online.

- High growth firms recruit twice as many new hires online as average growth firms.

- The level of online recruiting varies by industry.

- It is dangerous to assume that online marketing is not relevant to your industry.

- Online marketing budgets are rapidly increasing.

- The strength of your firm's brand (reputation and visibility) is directly impacted by online activity.

CASE STUDY
Modative Architects Finds 90% of Leads Online

Modative Architects boasts some impressive online marketing results:

- Approximately 90% of the firm's leads come through its website

- They receive about 4 leads per week online

- The firm's web traffic increased from 10 visits a week to 400 per day in a short period of time

How did they do it?

Find the Right Keyword Opportunity
Founder Derek Leavitt and his team were able to use search engine data to uncover some great keyword opportunities. They were careful to select terms that receive heavy search traffic but which don't appear on many websites. Often these are highly specific keyword phrases, such as "small lot subdivisions."

This is a niche keyword that they felt they could own. It accurately describes one of their core services, and it was ripe for the picking. Great. What next?

Create a Quality Content Piece with a Conversion Action
The Modative team wrote several pieces of educational content on the topic of small lot subdivisions. They packaged these pieces as "guides" and "packets" and posted them in the Resources section of their website for download.

These helpful content pieces are free, but they require an email address to download. The idea here is that when someone searches on a specific keyword phrase, they will click through to an appropriate resource page. If the content on the page is relevant, the visitor will supply their email address and download the piece.

Modative has taken this approach to heart and transformed its website into a lead generation machine. Check out their resources to see other examples of the same model.

How Does this Apply to Your Firm?
Start thinking about what types of educational content you could be producing for your web visitors. Not only will valuable content increase trust between you and your prospects, it will also drive web traffic and conversions.

★ THE SWEET SPOT ★

Finding the right mix of online and
offline marketing.

Just about any way you look at it, the case for online marketing is pretty compelling. Faster growth, greater profit, easier recruiting, increased brand awareness. What's not to like?

Yet there are lingering questions. For many firms, it's a jump into the unknown and unfamiliar. The range of online tools is daunting and growing almost every day, and many firms have only a vague understanding of any of them. What's more, the traditional approaches still work and are comfortable.

Like many firms, Hinge didn't start out with a grand vision for online marketing.

The result is often a mix of hesitation and halfhearted experimentation. In fact, that's where we started, ourselves.

Hinge's Online Marketing Story

Like many firms, Hinge didn't start out with a grand vision for online marketing. Of course, as a branding and marketing firm, we've always had a website, an online newsletter and a program of email marketing.

But our emphasis had always been on what we now think of as traditional face-to-face marketing. Networking events, referrals, public speaking, article publishing, board memberships and executive roundtables made up the core of our marketing plan.

Sure, we had a blog and were nominally on LinkedIn and Facebook, but our expectations and investment were very limited. The result was fairly predictable, at least in retrospect. We received a small proportion, less than 20%, of our leads from online sources. Our recruiting and brand building impacts were modest.

LON SAFKO
Author, *The Social Media Bible*

"Commenting on blogs is a highly effective method for reaching influencers. Similar to attending a business social event, you've got to get involved in the conversation. Add your own perspective and make your comments really count. Then influencers will begin to notice you."

Then everything changed. We decided to act on the results of our own research.

An Online Makeover

We recognized there was a relationship between online marketing and high growth in our research studies. And we had made a commitment to using empirical research to drive our marketing. So it became clear that we needed to make a major investment in our online activities.

While we continue to evolve our approach, we were struck by how fast we began seeing results. The first thing we noticed was that website traffic doubled. Then it doubled again and continues to grow to this day.

As we put more effort into our online marketing, new business leads began to grow. Best of all, the leads tended to be more qualified and were interested in the exact services that we offer.

We also noticed an increase in interest from potential new employees. And we started hearing from prospects and referral sources that our brand was gaining strength. We were encouraged and began to shift more of our resources from traditional marketing to our online efforts.

The first thing we noticed was that website traffic doubled.

The Results

The results opened our eyes. Wide open. In less than a year we went from generating less than 20% of our new business online to almost 70% today. This shift was accompanied by a sharp increase in our growth rate and a significant reduction in marketing expenses. And to our surprise, we began hearing from qualified prospects around the country. Today, we have clients from coast to coast, as well as in Europe and Canada. It's been quite a journey!

Growth is up, profits are up, online recruiting is up, and our brand strength is on the rise. In short, we have borne out the results of our research.

Those Two Questions Again

As we began to help clients make the same transition we had experienced ourselves, we heard the two big questions we raised in Chapter 4.

1. From a business perspective, what is the right level of investment in online marketing?

2. What is the right marketing approach for a professional services firm?

The second question will be the focus of the remainder of this book. But before we go there, let's tackle the first question.

Growth and Profitability

We'll begin by reviewing key financial results and their relationship to online marketing. When looking across all firms in all industries, our data clearly show that growth rate peaks when about half (40-60%) of leads are obtained from online sources (see Fig. 16). After that, it moderates but remains relatively high.

Fig. 16. Firm Growth, Profitability and Online Lead Generation Across All Industries

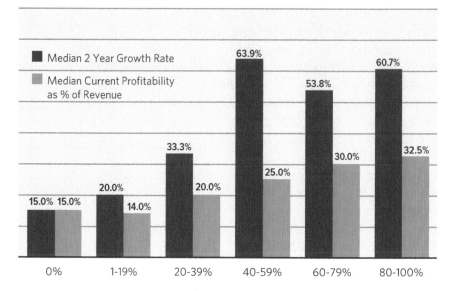

% **Leads Generated Online**

Profitability begins to improve once online lead generation exceeds 20%. And it continues to grow as online lead percentage increases.

So from a high-level perspective, the research points to the following scenarios:

- If you get no leads online, investing more should initially increase growth, then profitability.

- If you get 1-39% of your leads online, increased investment should accelerate growth and profitability.

- If you get 40% or more leads online, you may be able to trade higher growth for greater profitability by adjusting your level of investment.

There is significant pressure to increase investment just to stay even.

Competitive Pressure

From a competitive perspective there is also pressure to invest. Every industry that we studied is significantly increasing its online marketing budgets. Remember, two thirds of firms are, on average, increasing budgets by over 50%. High growth firms are planning even more aggressive expansion of their online budgets.

There is significant pressure to increase investment just to stay even. And remember: just because you're not getting business online doesn't mean your competitors aren't.

Return on Investment

If you find yourself wanting to project a specific return on investment, here is how to go about it. Begin by identifying your firm's current amount of online lead generation. Then look at the value of moving it to the next level of performance.

What is the economic impact of increasing your growth rate by 5% or 10%? What is the value of increasing profitability by 5 percentage points? In most cases, this will be a substantial number.

Let's take an example. Suppose you are a $20 million firm generating about 10% of your leads online and making a 15% profit. That produces a profit of $3 million.

Let's further suppose you intend to raise lead generation to a 20% level. That should increase both growth rate and profitability. So if we focus just on profitability, you could expect it to rise by 5 percentage points based on the percentages in Fig. 16. That would raise profitability from the current 15% to 20%. Profits would rise from $3 million to $4 million. That's a cool $1 million return on your investment.

So the ROI is likely to be very favorable.

You could make a similar projection for growth rate, as well. And the projected return would be very substantial. What about the costs? While our research doesn't answer that question directly, our experience is that your costs would likely be a small fraction of the return. So the ROI is likely to be very favorable.

Dangerous Dabbling

The real risk is not that you will spend too much. It's that you won't spend enough to make online lead generation successful. In fact, this is the most common mistake we see today.

Because firms new to online marketing are uncertain of the risks, they devote only minimal resources to the effort. The result, of course, is limited results. They may even conclude that it doesn't work. In short, they not only waste their initial investment, they draw the wrong conclusion, to boot.

From a business investment perspective, the strategy is clear. Invest enough to do it right or don't invest at all.

Should You Go All Digital?

Does it make sense to go completely digital and abandon all traditional marketing? While the numbers do make a compelling argument, we don't recommend an all-or-nothing approach for most firms.

Our research suggests that a balanced approach may be the most productive. That way, you can be everywhere your target clients are with a message that speaks to their needs.

Invest enough to do it right or don't invest at all.

That is the real beauty of online marketing. It helps you get in front of qualified prospects very efficiently and cost effectively. It does not replace face-to-face contact, but online marketing supports and complements it. It builds your reputation and extends your visibility.

Okay, online marketing sounds pretty great. How do you proceed? And what's the right way for a professional services firm like yours to approach online marketing? That's what we'll explore next.

Key Takeaways

- Many firms are cautious about investing in online marketing.

- From a growth and profitability perspective there is a compelling case to go digital.

- Competitive pressure also supports the business case.

- The greatest danger lies in underinvesting in online initiatives.

- The right answer for most firms is a balance of traditional and online marketing.

YOUR ONLINE MARKETING TOOLKIT: WHAT WORKS

★ EVALUATING THE TOOLS ★

Which tools drive success in the digital world?

E ven if you've concluded that online marketing makes sense for your firm, you are still faced with the daunting task of selecting and prioritizing the tools you should use. Well, you're in luck. We're about to do the hard work for you.

In this book we examine 15 common online marketing tools. For each of these we performed a three-stage analysis:

1. How do average firms and high growth firms use the tool?

2. How effective is the tool as judged by average and high growth firms?

3. How effective is the tool as evaluated by a panel of experts?

In this way, we hope to clear some of the confusion around the question of what works for driving professional services marketing success.

Tool Use in High Growth vs. Average Firms

Are high growth firms more likely to use blogging or webinars? Are average firms using LinkedIn more or less than high growth firms? These are the types of questions that our analysis can help you answer.

We asked each of the firms to rate the relative focus they placed on each of the online tools featured in our study. A rating of 0 indicated that they didn't use the technique at all. We then compared the ratings of the high grow firms to those of average firms (see Fig. 17).

Fig. 17. Focus Rating: High Growth vs. Average Firms

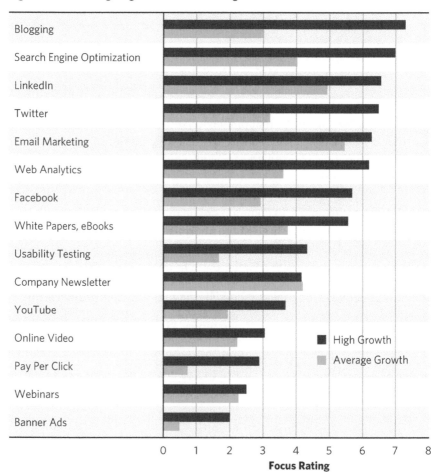

Notice the big differences in focus between high growth and average firms. With a few notable exceptions, high growth firms use online marketing tools more aggressively.

A notable exception to this trend is the use of e-newsletters, which are adopted at about the same level in both high growth and average firms. This is a tool that has been around for a long time and is quite widely used.

JENNIFER ABERNETHY

Author, *The Complete Idiot's Guide to Social Media Marketing*

Email marketing and webinars are used more intensely by high growth firms, but not by as wide a margin as other tools. In most other cases though, high growth firms are much more likely to embrace the online tool.

"In order to properly interact and develop relationships, you should spend at least an hour per day engaging. Taking 5 or 10 minutes to update your status is not enough to really make a difference."

Level of Use

Another striking feature of Fig. 17 is the wide range of tools used by firms. Blogging and SEO are heavily embraced by high growth firms. Pay-per-click advertising, webinars, and banner ads are used less.

Apart from common techniques such as email marketing and firm newsletters, social media tools account for some of the highest levels of adoption among average firms. Of course, just because something is widely used, doesn't necessarily mean it's effective. That's where we turn next.

Tool Effectiveness — High Growth vs. Average Firms

If a firm was using an online tool, we asked them to rate how effectively it helped them meet their business objectives. In this way, we could assess the impact of techniques even if they were not commonly used.

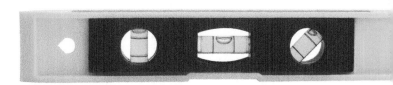

The results of this analysis provided some interesting surprises (see Fig. 18). With a few exceptions, high growth firms found almost all online tools more effective than their average growth counterparts. Only firm newsletters and webinars were rated similarly for effectiveness.

Fig. 18. Effectiveness Rating: High Growth vs. Average Firms

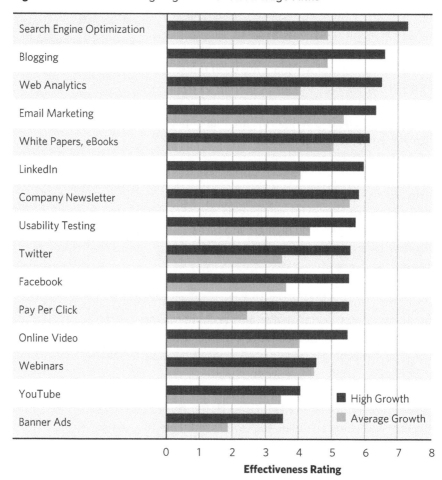

A few tools rose in the rankings when they were rated by effectiveness, compared to their usage ratings. Web analytics and pay-per-click advertising are two good examples of underappreciated tools. Social media tools tend to be somewhat overused relative to their effectiveness.

One way to interpret the results is that high growth firms are simply using these online tools more effectively. But is there even more to be gained? For that answer we turned to our expert panel.

How the Experts See These Tools

Do experts who specialize in these tools see even greater potential — beyond what the high growth firms in our study have experienced? To resolve this question we asked each expert to rate the effectiveness of each tool for professional services firms. We then compared their ratings to those of both high growth and average growth firms.

JIM BOYKIN
Founder & CEO, *Internet Marketing Ninjas*

"We favor organic to PPC, focusing the majority of our efforts on organic. PPC is great for targeting very specific terms, and for building up traffic before you have organic rankings. But overall, investing in organic SEO means investing in a long term strategy that builds momentum continually over time."

The results, shown in Fig. 19 (see next page), tell an interesting story. In most cases the answer was yes. Professional services firms are not yet realizing most of these tools' full potential.

While high growth firms were seeing better results than average firms, the experts see even more potential. This potential is greatest in some of the basic techniques such as SEO, web analytics and usability testing. They also identified additional potential in fundamental content marketing tools such as blogging, white papers, eBooks and webinars.

> Professional services firms are not yet realizing most of these tools' full potential.

Conversely, high growth firms noted greater efficacy than the experts in two tools: Facebook and banner ads.

Fig 19. Effectiveness Ratings: Experts vs. High Growth vs. Average Firms

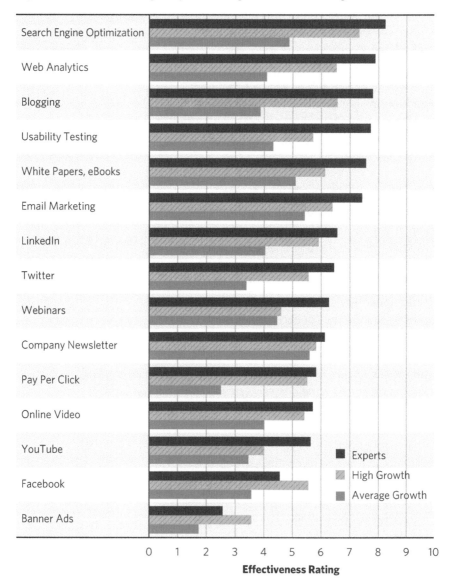

In the next chapter, we take a quick look at each of these tools and where they might fit into a structured marketing program.

Key Takeaways

- High growth firms use online marketing tools more aggressively.

- High growth firms also find online tools to be more effective.

- Search engine optimization, blogging and web analytics are rated as most effective.

- The experts see even greater potential in most of the techniques evaluated.

CASE STUDY
Xtivia's 5 Lead
Generation Strategies

XTIVIA

Xtivia, a technology solutions and services company, is driving approximately 40% of its leads from online sources. CEO Dennis Robinson heads an ambitious team of marketers that clearly understands the value of digital marketing. Here are five ways they generate leads from their website.

1. Crack the Adwords Code

There is no shortage of professional services firms that use Google Adwords pay-per-click advertising. But few firms understand how to do it right. Xtivia spends generously on Adwords, and they generate more than enough new business to justify the cost.

"People clicking on our ads are usually very targeted and qualified. They have a need, are looking for a service and are ready to act," explained Robinson. The firm routinely receives 5 to 10 inbound leads per week from pay-per-click campaigns, some of which result in multimillion-dollar projects.

2. Monitor Visitor Activity

Robinson and his team regularly evaluate how web visitors are interacting with the website. Using a service called LeadLander, they are alerted when visitors hit certain important pages.

The team also follows which keywords visitors are searching. A website's content should closely reflect what visitors are searching for. If it doesn't, visitors won't find what they are looking for and will quickly leave the site. The team tracks keyword quality by analyzing the amount of time visitors spend on the site for each keyword searched.

3. Never Stop Tweaking
The company's website is built on a content management system so they can easily make changes to their site. As the team monitors visitor activity, they can quickly tweak the website's content to be more effective.

According to Robinson, "Our website is a living, breathing entity. We are constantly trying different things, looking to maximize performance."

4. Respond Quickly
All leads come through Robinson first, and he ensures they receive responses within 15 minutes. "If you think you can wait a day, you're wrong," says Robinson. "If you sit there and wait, they've already found a competitor."

Xtivia employees know to "Stop, Drop, and Dial" when a prospect call or website form fill comes in.

5. Educate to Build Trust
The Xtivia blog builds trust, attracts new visitors and covers common questions about Xtivia services. The different technical teams work together to generate customer questions or hot topics. By writing blog posts that cover a wide variety of technical subjects, Xtivia is gradually building a library of thought leadership.

As people search Google for answers to commonly asked technology questions, they may be taken to a useful Xtivia blog post. Creating this content not only drives traffic to the website, it also nurtures prospects and develops relationships.

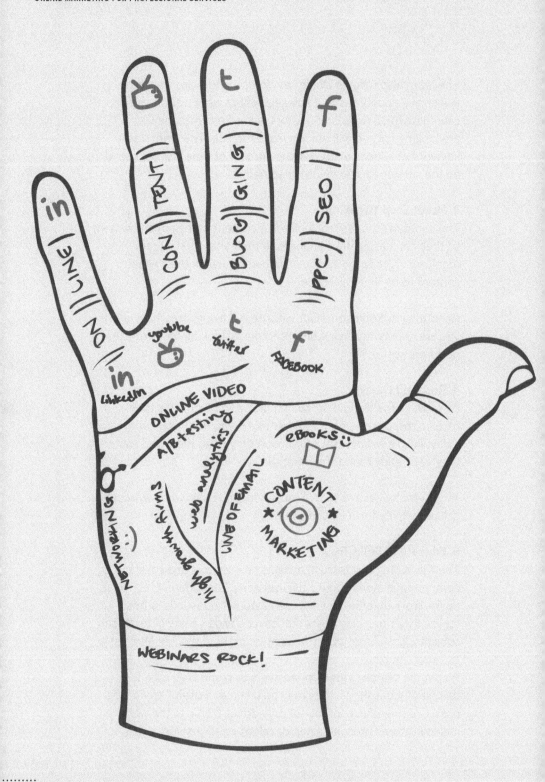

CHAPTER 9

★ YOUR ONLINE ★
MARKETING TOOLKIT

A roadmap for the world of online
marketing tools.

I f you feel overwhelmed by all of the online marketing options available to
you, don't despair. We wrote this chapter for you. If you are wondering
where to begin and how to assemble all the pieces in a coherent way,
we've got answers. After consulting our experts and observing what works
for high growth firms, we've put together some general guidelines to help
you prioritize your online marketing efforts.

We've organized the 15 online tools covered
in the study into six phases. These phases
generally reflect the priority and sequence
in which a typical professional services
firm might deploy the tools in an online
marketing strategy.

Phase 1: Build a Solid Foundation

These first two tools are fundamental to any successful online marketing program. Everything that comes later builds upon these platforms.

Search Engine Optimization (SEO)

What is this? - SEO (also called organic search) is a process that attracts traffic to your website from Google and other search engines and makes it easier for prospective clients to find you when searching on a wide range of relevant search terms. The process involves creating or editing content, making technical adjustments to your website and boosting your site's search engine authority by encouraging other websites to link to yours. Research is critical to SEO. It involves uncovering the keyword phrases that will draw qualified web searchers to your site.

Why do I need it? - More and more, businesses are using search engines to find and evaluate professional services. When you rank for relevant terms in your industry, you can attract interested, qualified visitors — people who may otherwise never find you — to your website.

When should I do it? - SEO is an ongoing process, but you should start working on it as soon as possible. Don't expect to see significant results for about three months. And because search engine algorithms change frequently, you will need to make adjustments over time.

Web Analytics

What is this? - Web analytics allow you to track visitor activity on your website, such as visits, downloads, form fills and traffic sources.

Why do I need it? - Analytics provide the insights you need to make adjustments to your marketing program. When you understand how visitors are interacting with your website, you can evaluate what's working and find ways to improve your site's performance. Without analytics, your online marketing is flying blind.

When should I do it? - Google Analytics, the world's most popular analytics software, is free. If you don't have it already, install it today and begin tracking your web traffic. Once you learn the basics — such as number of unique visitors, top content, top keywords and referral sources — try something a little more advanced. Set up goals you want to track (for example a contact form fill) and monitor its performance on a daily or weekly basis.

Phase 2: Create Valuable Content

The techniques in this phase help you build a library of content that will attract and convert potential clients. This content will become central to your online marketing program.

Blogging

What is this? - For our purposes, blogging is a way to publish fresh educational content to your website on a regular basis. Your blog should address topics of interest to your firm's target market, and many of the posts should be written with a keyword phrase in mind (see SEO, above).

Why do I need it? - When you write valuable content, you demonstrate your expertise and earn the trust of your readers. Each blog post will be indexed by search engines, which allows qualified, interested prospects to find your website. In addition, well-written content attracts links, which is a significant part of SEO.

DANNY DOVER
Author, *Search Engine Optimization Secrets*

"People focus too much on the specific details of how the search engines change and not enough on real people. You don't need to trick search engines. You should instead create truly valuable content focused on helping people. If you do that, you can perform well in search rankings without having to worry about a time when your tactics suddenly stop working."

When should I do it? – Start blogging as soon as you can afford the time and people it takes to do it on a regular basis (at least once a week). In-house marketing teams and top executives are typical bloggers, but blog writing can also be outsourced. This is a long-term initiative. It can take 6 months to a year before you see results.

White Papers, eBooks, Articles

What are these? – These are educational content pieces that you can make available for download on your website (and, potentially, elsewhere). These pieces are similar to blog content, but they are more substantial. While the differences between these formats is a little fuzzy, white papers tend to be more technical, articles are usually less formal and eBooks typically run longer than articles. Some firms require visitors to register before downloading substantive content, while others make these pieces freely available. Give registration a try, as many people are willing to trade a little personal information for a more valuable piece of content.

Why do I need them? – Offering in-depth educational pieces is a great way to cultivate trust and increase the visibility of your brand. They also provide an opportunity to collect email addresses and build a list that can be used later for email marketing. Along with your blog, these pieces will make up the core of your content library and enhance your firm's reputation as thought leaders.

When should I do them? – Once your blog has been up and running for three to six months, start planning a longer content piece, such as a white paper or eBook. By then you will have a better sense of what kinds of content resonate with your target audiences. Some firms produce pieces like this one or more times each month. Others produce them less frequently. Your rate of production will depend on your goals and the resources at hand.

 Online Video
What is this? – This is the process of producing and publishing videos on your firm's website and other distribution channels. Examples of videos include case studies, company overviews and service descriptions.

Why do I need it? – Video consumption is on the rise and web visitors want content that is easily digestible and engaging. When you tell your story through video it comes alive and can really resonate with viewers. Well-produced videos establish trust and lead to higher lead conversion rates. They are also helpful in SEO efforts.

GINNY REDISH
Author, *Letting Go of Words—Writing Web Content that Works*

"Website usability testing and analytics are necessary in understanding your audience. Learning how visitors are interacting with your website is arguably more important than any other online marketing tactic."

When should I do it? – When you have a complex story to tell or when you want to enhance your credibility, video is an ideal medium. It's also an excellent choice when you want to communicate your firm's personality when a face-to-face meeting is impractical. Videos with high productions values, however, can be fairly expensive to produce, so plan accordingly. There is, however, a place for less formal video, especially as part of a blogging program.

Phase 3: Nurture Your Audience
Use this group of tools to communicate with potential clients so that you can nurture, qualify and convert them.

 Email Marketing
What is this? – Cultivate a targeted list of contacts and periodically email them with educational content and relevant offers.

Why do I need it? – Email is a proven channel for reaching prospects and nurturing them throughout the buying process. To stay on top of your prospects' minds, encourage them to subscribe or opt-in to useful content such as industry reports, research findings or relevant case studies. Email marketing is not the same as spam email, which is a numbers game based on blasting people with untargeted business offers. Email marketing is even more powerful when paired with capable client relationship manager (CRM) software.

When should I do it? – Like blogging, you should begin email marketing once you have the resources to write valuable content. Some firms have success with a monthly email, while others with more resources achieve better results sending two or three emails per week.

Company e-newsletter

What is this? – E-newsletters come in a variety of formats (single article, multiple articles, news digests, etc.) and are delivered to recipients via email. Most are sent to opt-in lists, so the content can be highly targeted.

Why do I need it? – Including an e-newsletter subscription form on your website can be an effective way to build your email list. If the content you send is educational and valuable to subscribers, an e-newsletter is a proven way to nurture prospects.

When should I do it? – Produce an e-newsletter when you have the resources to write valuable content. Typical frequency is once or twice per month, though some are sent weekly.

Webinars

What is this? – Webinars are educational online presentations that you offer to a group of registrants. In a typical webinar, the audience watches the equivalent of a PowerPoint presentation while listening to the presenters speak. At the end, participants are usually encouraged to ask questions to the presenters.

Why do I need it? – Webinars, like live seminars, are big credibility builders. As an online teacher, you can easily build trust and nurture prospects. If executed properly, webinars often produce highly-motivated new business leads.

When should I do it? – Consider conducting webinars once you have a sizable email list. Try promoting and running one webinar and evaluate whether it's right for your firm. Many firms conduct webinars every couple of months, although some offer them monthly or even weekly. To get in front of a new audience, you may want to run a joint webinar with another firm or subject matter expert.

Phase 4: Promote Your Activities with Online Networking

You probably know these techniques as social media. In the context of marketing, they help you interact with people online to get your message out and drive interest in your firm. They are also useful when you have valuable content you want to promote.

LinkedIn

What is this? – LinkedIn is a social network dedicated to professionals. Members create profiles and can interact with others within specific business groups (called LinkedIn Groups).

Why do I need it? – LinkedIn can be used in many ways, including networking, promoting content and increasing brand visibility. By establishing relationships with group members in your industry, you create a channel for discussing issues and building your firm's reputation as thought leaders.

When should I do it? – Once you are able to create blog content consistently, LinkedIn gives you a place to share it. Join a few industry groups and begin joining the discussions. When appropriate, share links to your content pieces as support for your points. Expect to spend 30 minutes to an hour a day on LinkedIn if you are looking for a substantial presence.

Twitter

What is this? – Twitter is a micro-blogging platform that allows members to broadcast messages of up to 140 characters in length. It's often used for spreading industry news and spotting trends.

Why do I need it? – Twitter is an excellent platform for building relationships, sharing industry news and promoting your content. Once you have developed online relationships ("followers"), you'll be able to promote your blog posts, share content produced by others and generate buzz more easily.

When should I do it? – If you are consistently creating blog content, you should start spending time interacting with others on Twitter. Find members in your industry and begin to interact and share. Don't expect much from Twitter unless you can devote 30 minutes to an hour per day using it.

Facebook

What is this? – Facebook is the largest social network in the world. Facebook allows individuals and companies to maintain personal profiles and share information.

Why do I need it? – Unlike LinkedIn, Facebook is not specific to business, but it does boast a much larger base of members. Facebook is another channel to promote your content, interact with others in your industry and improve your firm's visibility. If your company Facebook page is interactive and updated frequently with valuable content, it can be a significant traffic generator for your website and helpful for recruiting.

When should I do it? – Like Twitter and LinkedIn, you should focus on Facebook once you have a solid stock of content and the resources to update the page and engage in with other Facebook users on a daily basis. If you spend 30 minutes to an hour per day, you should begin to see spikes in engagement and traffic.

YouTube
What is this? – YouTube is a platform for publishing and sharing videos. Members can subscribe to video channels, rate videos and track viewing activity. It is also the world's number 2 search engine.

Why do I need it? – Like Facebook, YouTube is a heavily trafficked social network that can lead to brand visibility. Use it to promote training videos, case stories and viral campaigns. If your firm is producing video, uploading those videos and promoting them on YouTube can generate significant buzz.

When should I do it? – When your firm begins producing video, create a YouTube channel and upload all your videos to one location. In the professional services realm, interacting and engaging other members on YouTube is generally secondary to LinkedIn, Twitter and Facebook.

Phase 5: Optimizing Performance

These sophisticated tools allow you to tune your website and landing pages for maximum performance.

Usability and A/B Testing

What are these? – These are two ways to optimize website visitor interaction and the performance of your site. Usability tests help you learn how individual users interact with and navigate your site. A/B tests deliver two versions of a web page to different visitors to determine which version performs better. A/B testing can also be used in email marketing to test different versions of an email.

Why do I need them? – Most web teams spend a lot of time debating how to structure a website or what to change in its design. In most cases, it's impossible to determine the optimal approach without testing the options in the real world. So test different pieces of your website. You'll learn empirically what is and isn't working. Then you can take steps to reduce friction on your website.

When should I do them? – If you are going to redesign your website, it's useful to test your existing site to see what works well and what doesn't. Insights from these tests will inform decisions for the new design. It is good practice, as well, to conduct tests periodically on your existing site to optimize landing pages and conversion pathways to your goals.

Phase 6: Pay for Performance

These more specialized techniques allow you to pay for increased visibility and web traffic.

Pay Per Click (PPC)

What is this? – Pay per click is an advertising channel typically associated with Google's Adwords program. You post an advertisement in the sidebar or top area of relevant Google search results and pay a small fee each time the ad is clicked.

Why do I need it? – PPC advertising can be a valuable supplement to organic (unpaid) search engine traffic. It should not, however, replace organic SEO entirely. Use PPC when you need to generate additional web traffic quickly or when you want to target a keyword term for which you don't (or can't) rank organically. Resulting traffic has the potential to be very targeted and high quality because the advertiser (you) is in control of keyword selection.

When should I do it? – Run a PPC campaign when you have a specific offer you are trying to promote. Google Adwords allows you to send traffic to specific landing pages, making PPC a reliable way to drive conversions for a campaign.

Banner Ads

What is this? – These allow you to display a graphical advertisement on a third-party website. A banner ad can be a static image or a brief animation. The ad will also include a succinct message and will link to either a landing page or your website.

Why do I need it? – Banner advertising can be effective when you want to become more visible or promote an important piece of content to a specific online audience.

When should I do it? – If you want to increase visibility among a certain audience, target specific websites and carefully track your click-through rate. Banner ads may work for carefully targeted, easy-to-communicate offers.

For an average firm looking to grow, almost all of the tools described in this chapter offer significant potential. But how do they fit together into an overall marketing program?

That's up next.

Key Takeaways

- Online marketing is within reach, even to mere mortals.

- Begin with the fundamental building blocks — search engine optimization, web analytics and great content — before tackling more advanced techniques.

- These tools work together, and each one adds greater depth to your marketing program.

CASE STUDY
How Freed Maxick Uses Social Marketing to Drive Revenue

Trust earned.

CPA powerhouse Freed Maxick generates 20 to 30 percent of its annual new business revenue from online sources, including social media, search engines, mobile and its website. The firm's Marketing Director, Eric Majchrazak, explained how they navigate the world of accounting marketing.

A Different Look at Social Marketing

Sure, Eric and his team have a solid understanding of search engine optimization, email marketing and other online marketing fundamentals. But what impressed us was the way Freed Maxick uses social media to attract prospects.

Eric spends an hour or two each day scouring the net for relevant conversations. Using tools such as Google Alerts and Twitter search, he's able to focus on specific groups of people that may need his firm's help. For example, he may search twitter for a relevant term, such as "recommend accountant."

The results lead him to real-time conversations between people who are using that phrase. Instantly, Eric finds himself standing next to (virtually, of course) a potential client. He jumps into the discussion, adds valuable comments and initiates a relationship — one that may grow over time.

Using these same tools, the Freed Maxick team will also search for "trigger events." A trigger event might be a new product launch or the sale of a building. Often someone involved in these events needs tax and accounting help. By tracking discussions on these topics, Eric and his team are constantly at the right place at the right time, ready to step in and offer a helping hand.

Think Social is a Joke? Think Again.
Most executives think social media is about updating status messages and pushing out content. But there is much, much more to social marketing.

Don't turn your back on the online world. Between search and social, there is a tremendous opportunity to connect with your target audience — anywhere in the world. It's a matter of figuring out the most effective ways to put these tools to work at your firm. If you want to push your firm's growth, take your cue from Freed Maxick and begin exploring the social side of accounting marketing.

PLANNING YOUR ONLINE MARKETING ENGINE

How online marketing tools work together
to achieve your goals.

F or many professional services executives and marketers, the sheer number of available online tools can be pretty intimidating. After all, every time you turn your head something new has come to market. So where should you focus your attention? What's most important? How can you translate online activity into business?

Firms can establish trust by engaging their audience online.

We've found it's best to start with a model that shows how the tools work together. We'll call this model your online marketing engine.

Building Trust Through Engagement

One of the key characteristics of professional services business relationships is trust. Historically that trust has been built on face-to-face interaction over time. But as we discussed in Chapter 3, there is a new way to build that trust. Today, firms can establish trust by engaging their audience online.

BRYAN EISENBERG

Author, *Waiting for Your Cat to Bark?*

"Leads lose effectiveness by a factor of 6x within the first hour of not being responded to. I recommend tracking when a lead came in, when the first interaction was with a real human being, and every other touch point along the way. Optimizing your lead nurturing process can significantly affect your closing percentage."

This engagement can happen in a variety of ways — reading the content you produce or interacting directly with your firm online. But it almost always takes great content to stimulate engagement.

An Eye Opener

An experience we had at our own firm nicely illustrates this process. A professional services firm in our local area asked us to submit a proposal for a significant amount of work. We asked if they wanted to meet with us first, but they said they didn't need to. They were already very familiar with us because they had followed us and our work online for some time.

We were skeptical, but we submitted a proposal. Weeks went by, then one day we got a call. They were ready to get started — no meeting needed! But that wasn't half the story.

Only later did we learn that they had conducted a full search, including rounds of face-to-face interviews with other potential firms. Why did they retain us? Because they had developed a level of familiarity and trust based on our online presence that made face-to-face interaction unnecessary.

> The main reason people are coming is to access the content you are sharing.

This story is not unique. As we write these words, two of our last three new clients are firms we've never met in person.

Now, don't get us wrong. Face-to-face networking is still a valuable way to develop business. But it's not the only way. To show you what we mean, let's take a look at our model.

The Online Marketing Engine Model

Fig. 20 is a blueprint of how an online marketing engine works. The steps represent the different levels of engagement. At the lowest level is anonymous online traffic. Most often, this is traffic to your website. And the main reason people are coming is to access the content you are sharing.

Fig. 20. Online Marketing Engine Model

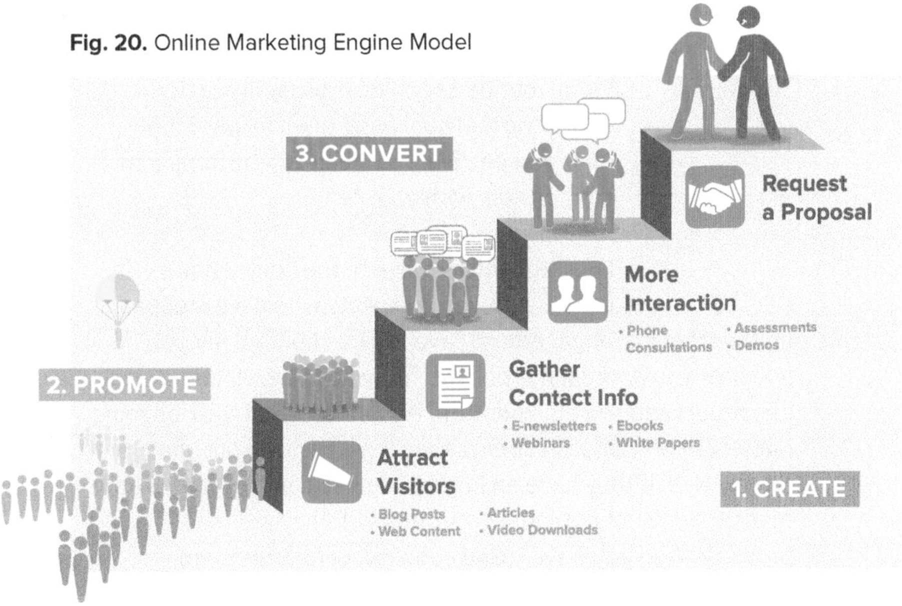

Whether your content consists of blog posts, articles, infographics, videos or slides, much of it is made freely available to encourage people to explore, read and engage. There is no registration required to view this content. And within this open access content there are offers for additional valuable content, such as eBooks, webinars, white papers, guides, kits and e-newsletters.

This content provides more in-depth coverage of issues, so it's perceived as more valuable. For this reason, readers are more willing to trade contact information for it through a simple registration form. They are willing to step up the level of engagement because they have begun to trust you. And if the exchange is a fair one — the content meets their expectations — you will increase the level of trust.

Moving Up

Embedded in the information you provide, or in follow-up communications, are additional offers. These offers promote other kinds of content that increase engagement further. Examples might include free assessments or reviews, workshops or product demos. For prospects that have a genuine interest or need, these forms of engagement are a natural and welcome step.

> Great content fuels the online marketing engine.

From your perspective, prospects are both educating and qualifying themselves. From their perspective, prospects are becoming more comfortable with your firm.

Next, the offers move to the "request a proposal" level. Prospects who have stepped up the ladder of engagement have learned about what you do and how you approach problems. They have developed a level of comfort and trust in your firm. And, because of their ongoing interest in very specific topics, they have partially qualified themselves. If they have an immediate need, you probably have made their list of potential firms. In short, they are ready for a proposal. And you have rolled out a red carpet for them.

Content at the Core

To work, this model requires a certain amount of valuable content. That content must include pieces targeted at low levels of engagement, such as blog posts or videos, that require no registration or commitment to consume.

To capture leads, you need a stable of more valuable content, such as webinars, ebooks or topic-specific guides. Finally, you need content that requires more engagement but delivers even greater value.

Now, that's a lot of content — but boy is it worth it! Great content fuels the online marketing engine. As you may recall from Chapter 9, content tools were highly ranked by high growth firms and the expert panel. So how is this valuable content developed?

Figs. 21-23 show that great content is based on three things: 1) an understanding of your target client's challenges; 2) an understanding of online visitors' behavior (web analytics); and 3) SEO plays an important role in content, especially as you attract new readers at the lowest level of engagement. By making your open-access content keyword rich you help interested visitors find your writings and website through online search.

Fig. 21. Content Creation

JAMES BESWICK

Author, *Ranking Number One*

"On a scale from 0-10, publishing content is a 10. If you want to generate quality search engine traffic then you need to be writing quality content."

Speaking of attracting online visitors, let's talk about promotion.

Promoting Your Content

Once you have developed valuable content at various levels of engagement, how do you promote it? That's where a number of online and offline tools come in handy.

Fig. 22 shows that promotion involves search, both organic and paid. You may recall the very high level of effectiveness that high growth firms and online marketing experts place on SEO. In the hands of a skilled marketer, SEO is a very cost-effective way to generate well-targeted visitors to your site.

Social media also plays a useful role. Sharing your content on Twitter, LinkedIn and other platforms — and having conversations around relevant issues — builds familiarity and trust.

Fig. 22. Promoting Content

Email and e-newsletters are also useful ways to get your content in front of the right people. This is particularly true when it comes to the nurturing part of the relationship. You will want to share valuable content on a regular basis so that over time folks move up to higher levels of engagement.

> The better your content, the easier it is to promote.

Finally, consider finding partners that can extend your reach. These might be online sites that promote certain types of content, such as white papers, infographics, research reports or videos. Or they might be trade associations, industry specific networking groups, bloggers, trade publications or marketing partners from other firms trying to reach the same audience. By sharing your useful content, they bring more value to their constituents. In return, you raise your firm's profile and creditability. Of course, the better your content, the easier it is to promote.

Converting Visitors

As we looked at the components of the online marketing engine, we've mentioned using offers to convert visitors to the next level of engagement. Offers are critical components of the marketing engine, propelling prospects through the marketing pipeline until they become clients. No conversions, no clients.

In Fig. 23 (next page) you can see that several online marketing tools play an important role. This is one of the places where A/B testing, usability testing and web analytics earn their very high effectiveness ratings.

These tools help you optimize your offers and landing pages to maximize conversions. Because so few professional services firms understand or

MICHAEL FLEISCHNER
Author, *SEO Made Simple*

"Understand keyword research. If you can find keyword phrases that define a key aspect of your firm with high search volumes and little competition, you can gain an advantage over your competitors."

Fig. 23. Converting with Content

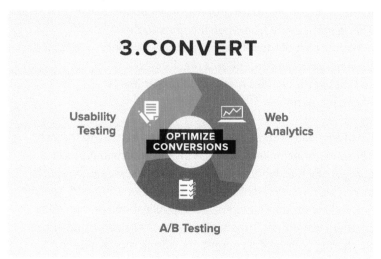

For most firms an outside marketing partner is a must.

use these sophisticated techniques, they are a great way for any firm willing to master them to gain a tangible competitive advantage. Usability testing, web analytics and A/B testing are the secret weapons of online marketing.

The Implementation Challenge

Once your marketing engine is in place, it can have a dramatic impact on the growth and profitability of the entire firm. The results of our research were as clear as they were compelling. But standing up the model can be a big job. And many specialized talents are required.

For many firms, an outside marketing partner is part of the solution. So how do you go about selecting one? That's where we pick up in the next chapter.

Key Takeaways

- Online marketing can build trust by incrementally increasing levels of engagement.

- The online tools work together to produce a very powerful marketing engine.

- Your online marketing engine has different levels of valuable content at its core.

- Your content is promoted in multiple ways and attracts visitors.

- Higher-value content requires registration and is used to generate leads.

- Over time, escalating engagement converts leads into qualified opportunities.

STEP-BY-STEP
IMPLEMENTATION

CHOOSING YOUR ONLINE
MARKETING PARTNER

Selecting the right marketing partner
can accelerate your results.

So far so good. You've evaluated the online marketing tools and are beginning to grasp the types of content you will need to create. So how and where do you get started?

Your firm is filled with experienced business and technical professionals. You may even have internal marketing staff. Your instincts say, "We can figure it out!" But when you sit down with all the players and look at the logistics, the level of effort to sustain a content marketing program just isn't in the cards.

Even when you know you need help, it's not easy to find the best marketing partner to assist you. What do you do?

Why it's hard to go it alone

Most professional services executives are already overextended, so how are they supposed to manage a content-heavy marketing program? We understand. We've been there. When you have to choose between meeting client deadlines and implementing your own marketing, the client always wins.

Even if you've got internal marketing staff, chances are they don't have the knowledge to run an efficient SEO campaign or the combination of subject matter expertise and writing skills to produce all that content. And while it's not impossible to do it all internally, it's going to be tough to keep up the momentum in the face of other competing priorities. That's why many firms look for a partner to ease the burden.

Partnering Options

The right marketing partner can accelerate your business results. They'll need to be flexible enough to work with you on an ongoing basis. And you'll want a firm that responds quickly when an opportunity arises.

When selecting an online marketing partner, consider how much time your firm can contribute to a content marketing program and how much you will need to outsource. Assuming you aren't able to handle the entire load yourself, you are left with three options, which we describe below.

Option	Level of Your Involvement	Level of Online Marketing Partner Involvement	Cost
1. Full outsourcing	Low	High	$$$$
2. Shared responsibility	High to Medium	Medium to High	$$$
3. Expert advice	High	Low to Medium	$$

Option 1: Full outsourcing – You hand over the entire program to an outside expert, ideally a marketing firm that not only knows online marketing but also knows your industry. You will be involved in the initial strategy and will approve campaigns and content along the way. But for the most part your firm will be free to focus on your core expertise and serving your clients. Your marketing partner should be able to provide regular reports, making it easy to track your progress.

Pros:

- Allows you to focus on serving your clients

- Increases the probability of success because critical tasks are handled by an expert

- Marketing staff doesn't have to learn as they go

- More likely the program will stay on schedule

- Reporting and analysis makes it easy to track progress

Cons:

- More expensive up front (though this cost could be offset by a better return)

- May require a higher level of buy-in from internal staff and leadership

- Less opportunity for internal staff to learn the skills needed to maintain the program over time

WILLIAM ALBERT

Author, *Measuring the User Experience*

"It depends on the organization, but firms that typically outsource website usability testing do so because they either don't have the expertise or they don't have the time. In order to receive an open and honest assessment without internal politics, it makes sense to hire a professional."

The right marketing partner can accelerate your business results.

Option 2: Shared responsibility – You get the guidance and expertise of a marketing firm, but you save cost by doing some of the work yourself. The marketing partner will work closely with your team to define the strategy and will handle tasks that your team doesn't have the skills or manpower to carry out. The marketing firm may also train your staff to execute certain tasks themselves. How much you spend under this arrangement depends on how much of the load your team can bear.

Pros:
- Costs less than a full outsourcing program

- Provides professional guidance

- Gives staff an opportunity to learn the ropes from experts so that they will be able to handle certain tasks unassisted in the future

- May provide reporting and analysis to track progress

Cons:
- Puts added pressure on already fully-burdened internal staff

- Because staff tend to focus on immediate client needs, the marketing program is more likely to get off schedule

Option 3: Expert advice – The marketing firm plays only a high-level role, offering advice and assistance as needed. Depending on the nature of the arrangement, it could also be involved in setting the marketing strategy. Your team takes on the responsibility for designing and implementing the plan, as well as monitoring its progress and making any needed mid-course adjustments. To keep client-related distractions from derailing your plan, you'll need to dedicate one or more employees to executing the program.

Pros:

- Minimal outside costs

- You have an expert resource to consult whenever you have questions or need advice

- Your team learns to execute the entire plan

Cons:

- You'll need dedicated internal staff to ensure the plan stays on track

- High likelihood that the program will not stay on schedule

- If a skilled marketing staff member leaves, it can put your whole program in jeopardy

- Your staff will be learning as they go, so it may take much longer to see results

- If your staff lacks specialized expertise, your program is less likely to achieve optimal results

Ten questions to ask your potential online marketing partner

In our study, *Professional Services: How Buyers Buy*, we discussed the three primary criteria of the buyer.[4]

- Can they solve my problem?

- Will they make my life easier?

- Do I like them?

4 http://www.hingemarketing.com/library/article/how_buyers_buy_professional_services_
buyers_study

To address these basic criteria, we've compiled a list of ten questions to help you evaluate a potential partner.

1. Do they walk the talk? In other words, do they actually use the techniques they recommend for you?

2. Do they have experience with your industry? Do they have the depth of knowledge to write lots of content that will resonate with your clients?

3. Are they listening and asking clarifying questions? If they aren't listening now, they probably won't later.

4. Will you get a solution specific to your needs or a generic solution? And how will it be tailored?

5. Who performs the actual work? Can you meet them?

6. Are they a big, generalist firm or do they specialize in the services you need?

7. How well do they understand the intersection of offline and online marketing?

8. Will they set concrete goals and measure their progress against them?

9. Can they help you anticipate where online marketing efforts stumble internally?

10. What role, if any, will a contact database (whether a simple Excel spreadsheet or a sophisticated CRM) play in an online marketing plan?

Location, Location, Location

What about the firm's physical location? Wouldn't it be easier to work with a local firm?

With the technology now available — video conferencing, chat, email — you don't need to sit down together in your conference room to get to know a potential partner. In fact, it's a lot easier to schedule impromptu meetings when one party doesn't have to factor in travel time. It's more important to find an expert that understands your business — wherever they are — than a less qualified provider in your city.

Online marketing is more sophisticated than traditional marketing. So it's important to use the best talent you can find. After all, the future of your firm is at stake. But whether you handle your marketing yourself or outsource it, you'll waste all that time and money if you don't follow the right strategy.

And that's where we're headed in Chapter 12.

Key Takeaways

- When your clients take priority, your marketing plan does not.

- Internal staff that do not run online marketing on a daily basis are not likely to have the skills to deliver an effective and consistent program.

- The right marketing partner is one that is flexible and responsive to your needs.

- Decide what level of outside help you need: full outsourcing, shared responsibility or high-level expert advice.

- Location is the least important criteria to consider when selecting an online marketing partner.

CASE STUDY
How One MEP Firm is Launching an Online Marketing Initiative

GHT, a Mechanical, Electrical and Plumbing (MEP) firm based outside of Washington, DC, in Arlington, Virginia, has cultivated a strong offline presence and reputation over its 45-year history. But they did not have much visibility online. Their website was eight years old and not getting any younger. And the firm was not doing any social media. So in the past year they made the decision to make a serious investment in online initiatives.

3, 2, 1, Liftoff

To launch their new marketing program, GHT looked first at their website. "Our website was out of date, static and brochure-like," said Ami Kelly, GHT's Director of Marketing and Business Development. "It conveyed an image that no longer fit our firm." So they rebuilt the site from the ground up on a content management system, allowing them to feature their latest work and optimize the site for online search and lead generation.

The firm's web partner conducted extensive keyword research to identify the best opportunities to raise GHT's profile in valuable Google search results. Within a month of the site's launch, it began ranking for important keyword phrases, including first position rankings for critical local search terms, such as:

- MEP Consultants Washington DC

- MEP Engineering Services Washington DC

- LEED Commissioning Washington DC

- Building Energy Services Washington DC

- MEP Consulting Washington DC

Two months later, web traffic was up 47% over the previous site. And as a result of a Google search by the editor of *PM Engineer,* GHT was featured in the magazine's March 2012 cover story.

Lead by Example

Once the new site had launched, Kelly began rolling out a new marketing strategy that centered on the new website. She took steps to encourage people throughout the firm to get involved. She wanted to leverage GHT's offline reputation as MEP experts to position the firm as industry thought leaders. The firm created a section on their website called Insights, where they publish their blog, white papers and video. In addition, Kelly and her team are active on social media.

With a new website in place and a steady stream of content the firm is already getting increased traffic and leads. From SEO to video production to blogging to social media, GHT is making the most of online marketing to connect with new prospects on the Internet.

CHAPTER 12

GETTING THE
★ STRATEGY RIGHT ★

Why strategy is important.

Your online marketing engine is made up of many moving pieces. To get the highest performance from your engine, you're going to have to make some important decisions up front. What will you firm look like in the next few years? Who will your clients be? Are you willing to make some fundamental changes to achieve your goals? And what are those goals, anyway?

Answers to basic questions like these will shape your online marketing strategy.

What type of firm do you want to be?
When working through your firm's strategy, start with the 10,000-foot view. Picture your firm in 5 years, 10 years and 15 years. Then try to answer these high-level questions:

- Is fast growth a priority? Not all firms have high growth on the agenda. But if you're looking to increase year-over-year revenues by 40, 50 or maybe even 100%, you'll need to craft your online marketing approach with this goal in mind.

ANN HANDLEY
Author, *Content Rules*

"You might see immediate results, but the richest payoff has a longer-term view. Content is a commitment, not a one-and-done campaign, so you must get out of the campaign mentality. As you create and distribute educational or entertaining or interesting content, you will gradually nurture a following of loyal subscribers."

• Are you competing nationally or locally? Your online marketing approach depends on your geographic aspirations. As search technologies become more and more targeted, it's crucial to decide whether you're attacking one city, a region or the whole country. Heck, even the world is within reach!

• How visible do you need to be to succeed? Is part of your strategy to be in the spotlight? Do you want to be known as a thought leader? Or do you prefer to be a niche expert that targets a narrow group?

The answers to these questions will help you prioritize your marketing efforts.

Understand your target client

To help you think strategically about your marketing, you need to define and understand your target client. Your ideal client may be a little different than the typical client you serve today, so ask yourself a few more questions.

Who is your ideal client? Are you targeting multiple industries? Or multiple roles within a company?

What topics and issues are these audience members interested in?

Where are these people spending their time? Are they on LinkedIn? If so, which groups do they belong to? Are there influential blogs that your audiences read on a regular basis?

How do they want to be reached? Do they prefer monthly newsletters or weekly blog posts? Do they read white papers or watch webinars?

These aren't easy questions to answer. So it can be helpful to develop personas for your main audience groups. Some marketers even give their personas human names. By creating these thumbnail profiles you can start to visualize the three or four types of people you will target with your marketing.

Example Persona 1: George the CEO

George is a top-level executive with decision-making power. He is interested in growing his company quickly and capturing more market share. He doesn't use social media, but he does subscribe to educational e-newsletters to stay on top of trends and issues. George has limited time so he can't be bothered with daily updates or marketing messages. Most of the time, George delegates any online research to his staff.

Example Persona 2: Vanessa the Marketing Manager

Vanessa is involved with the day-to-day operations of the marketing team. She doesn't have final say on major expenditures, but her voice is being heard within the organization. She spends an hour a day on Twitter and Facebook, and stays up to date on current events by reading three or four industry blogs.

By sketching out these personas, you can begin to see how different audiences might be more receptive to certain marketing tactics. It's your job to define your firm's segments and fully understand how each type of person can best be reached. As you create personas, you may find it helpful to model them after some of your clients — folks who fill these roles in real life.

Target client research

The best way to get inside the minds of your target clients is to ask them questions. Set up a few one-on-one interviews with clients and prospects to give you the insights you need to plan your strategy. From these interviews, you should learn:

- The most significant challenges your prospects are facing

- How your prospects want to be marketed to

- Types of content they subscribe to, read or watch

- Who they consider your competitors

- What they see as your firm's greatest value

Read about it. Research it. Master it.

What you'll likely find is that the external perceptions expressed in the interviews do not necessarily align with your firm's internal thinking or assumptions. This misalignment, of course, is what you are after. It gives you the insight to prepare a strategy that exploits real-world opportunities and resonates with your audiences. No more guessing what your prospects and clients want and need.

While you can conduct these interviews yourself, you are more likely to get honest answers if an impartial third party makes the calls for you. People are more inclined to open up and volunteer valuable perspectives if they don't have to worry about stirring the pot.

If you want to learn more about setting your strategy, check out Chapters 9 and 10 of our book *Spiraling Up: How to Create a High Growth, High Value Professional Services Firm*.

Understand client issues

If you do your research, you should have a pretty good idea of what your audiences care about. At this point, it's your job to become an expert in these issues.

Let's suppose you're an IT firm and your clients and prospects are interested in cloud security. It will benefit you to become a trusted thought leader in cloud security. Read about it. Research it. Master it. Then let the world know that you own the topic. This can be done by writing about the topic frequently on your blog, writing eBooks, presenting webinars, and spreading the word in social media.

If you live and breathe the issues your audience members care about most, they will begin to see you as an authority. Then when they are ready to buy, they'll go to the firm they trust — yours!

ERIC ENGE
Co-Author, *The Art of SEO*

"For professional services firms, focus on the homepage first. This is your highest priority. After securing initial rankings, focus 50% of your efforts on the homepage and 50% on sub services pages."

Keyword research

There is another way to discover what prospects and clients care about: search engine data. Using free software, such as the Google Keyword Tool, you can determine how often (more or less) people are searching for a given word or phrase.

You can use this data to determine what people are looking for online — and that gives you a pretty fair understanding of what topics folks are interested in. Then you can adjust your messaging and content to be more relevant to your audiences.

When writing content for your website and blog, you'll want to incorporate popular words and phrases into your text.

Your content will be much more likely to appear in Google's search results, which in turn pushes more qualified traffic to your website.

BRAD GEDDES

Author, *Advanced Google Adwords*

"The time it takes to see SEO results depends on the competitiveness of the industry. In a less competitive space you should start to see results in a month or two. In a competitive space, you're looking at three or four months."

Identify your primary services

When working through your marketing strategy, clearly define which core services you are selling. This may sound obvious, but many firms jump into online marketing without linking it to their ultimate goal, making the sale.

You can write hundreds of blog posts on trendy topics. You can attract thousands of new visitors. But if none of them convert into new business, you've wasted your time. Big traffic numbers can be deceiving. At the end of the day, people need to understand what you do or they won't ever think to hire you.

So if you are going to write a newsletter, make sure it relates to your offerings in some way. If you are going to spend time writing white papers and articles, be sure they attract the right types of visitors. And if you set a goal to increase your social followers and subscribers, monitor your following to ensure it includes folks in your target market—people that might conceivably buy your core services.

Understand the competitive environment

Competitive research might be the best way to figure out what online activities to focus on. On a high level, competitive research should be conducted with three goals in mind.

1. Discovering what others in your industry are doing online

2. Determining which tactics are working and which are not

3. Copying the best ideas from your competitors then figuring out how to do them better

Whether you're brainstorming keywords, writing an ad or finding a way to leverage your YouTube page, don't be afraid to look around to see what's already being done. Online marketing is not about reinventing the wheel. It's about understanding what works in your industry.

Big traffic numbers can be deceiving.

Fire up your web browser. Go to your competitors' websites. Then be on the lookout for these elements:

- Web design features, layout, imagery

- Company messaging and positioning

- Use of social media tools

- Keywords and phrases

- Use of content such as downloadable books and guides

- Offers

- Blog topics

It's about understanding what works in your industry.

Some of your competitors will be less evolved than you, and their websites will feel pretty dated and thin. Others will be savvier. Focus on the sites that seem to "get it." Some of your competitors will be soliciting leads online. Find them and figure out how they are doing it. These insights will help you to decide where to focus your efforts.

Document your online marketing strategy
We can't stress this point enough. Write your strategy down. The act of writing will force you to think methodically, and it will put your marketing team on the same page. Literally. Your strategy should include:

- High-level goals for the firm over the next year

- Specific goals your online marketing program will achieve in the next 12 months

- A breakdown of your target clients and their personas

- A list of target client issues and keywords

- The core services you are selling (keep this list short)

- Competitive analysis

- A detailed list of marketing initiatives that will allow you to achieve your goals

- How you will measure your results and how often you will report on them

- Priorities for the first quarter

- A 12-month budget

This is a living document, one that will evolve over the year. As you measure results, expect to tweak the strategy to optimize the program's performance.

Okay, you've got a strategy. How do you bring it down to earth and turn it into a finely-tuned marketing engine?

That's up next!

Key Takeaways

- Without a strategy, you will never know if your marketing works.

- It's important to identify what you are selling and who your target audiences are.

- Research of various types will form the foundation of your strategy.

- Write down your strategy so that it can be shared and revised over time.

FIRING UP YOUR MARKETING ENGINE

★ ★

Online marketing, from top to bottom.

U ntil you picked up this book, you probably thought your website was just a place where interested folks learned about your firm. By now, however, you probably suspect it should be more than that. And right you are. It's time to think of your website as a bustling online marketing hub where people discover and consume valuable content — a place where visitors return again and again for information and where, eventually, they decide to pay for your expertise.

Your website should attract visitors from all manner of sources: search engines, social media sites, partners' sites and scores of blogs and assorted sites that link to your content. Once people have found your hub, you can nurture them and build relationships. That's how a well-oiled marketing engine hums. But first you need to retool your website.

JUSTIN CUTRONI
Author, *Google Analytics*

"For 95% of the population Google Analytcs is sufficient for tracking web analytics. You can supplement this data by also looking at social media data. For the typical professional services firm, you won't need to invest in expensive analytics software."

The high performance website

Today, most professional services still produce static, brochure-style websites. These sites don't give visitors much reason to stick around or come back in the future. That's got to change.

If you intend to take advantage of online marketing to publish and promote valuable content, you need to develop what we call a high performance website. Your content should contain keywords (to capture traffic from search engines), be relevant to your target audience and relate in some way to your core service offerings. You will also need to share this content widely in appropriate social groups.

Firms that commit to this process over time attract more web traffic from search engines and social media and build a base of loyal subscribers. Did you know, for instance, that companies that blog get 55% more web traffic and 70% more leads than those that don't?[5]

Once visitors are on your site, you can begin to nurture them. A great way to do this is to provide offers on the website that lead them gradually up the sales funnel. An example of a low-commitment offer for new visitors, for instance, might be an invitation to sign up for your newsletter (in exchange for an email address). For visitors with more substantive needs, you might want to provide a prominent "Request a Proposal" offer. Tracking how many people convert on these offers and where they come from will give you a good indication of how well your website is performing. Properly configured, Google Analytics (or similar packages) can provide this information.

Valuable content is the fuel for the online marketing engine.

5 *http://www.hubspot.com/*

High Performance Website Mini Checklist:

☐ Are your homepage, services pages and other important subpages optimized for search engines?

☐ Are your blog posts optimized for SEO and easy social sharing?

☐ Do you have a library of white papers, eBooks, research studies and other valuable pieces that visitors can either freely read or access through a simple registration process?

☐ Do your pages have offers (also called "calls to action") that invite visitors to take a specific action, such as download a white paper or request a proposal?

☐ Have you installed an analytics package for tracking web traffic and offer conversions?

Valuable content

Valuable content is the fuel for the online marketing engine. Without it, nobody will come to your website, and you will struggle to generate online leads. So let's take a few moments to make sure you understand what we are talking about.

> Once visitors are on your site, you can begin to nurture them.

You hear the word content thrown around quite a bit these days. And it means different things to different folks. In the context of content marketing for professional services firms, it's helpful to break content into three buckets:

1. **Static Web Page Content –** This is the text on a firm's home page, services pages, industries pages, and other high-level web pages. In other words, content like that on your original brochure-style website.

2. **Stock Educational Content –** Longer, more evergreen pieces, such as eBooks, research reports, guides, kits and white papers.

3. **Flow Educational Content –** Blog posts are the most common type of flow content. This content is short and sweet — quickly digested by people searching the web or navigating the noisy world of social media. Flow content can even consist of stock content that is broken up into bite-sized pieces.

JOE PULIZZI

Co-Author, *Get Content Get Customers*

"A blog is the simplest way to distribute content on a regular basis. It is the center of your content generation and the repository of your thought leadership. A blog is a proven way of increasing brand visibility and generating leads."

These three types of content each play a vital role in the online marketing process. Flow content is essential for attracting people to your website — your online marketing hub. It's also a great way to keep people coming back. Stock content is then used to nurture visitors and convince them to convert on a download offer. Your static web page content helps visitors late in the buying process to learn more about your firm's credentials, offerings and background.

Your online community

"We've written tons of valuable content. So now what do we do?" Well, you still need to promote it. Yes, over time you will begin to attract web visitors through search engines. But if you rely solely on Google search you will miss out on a lot of valuable exposure.

To promote your content and your brand, it helps to find the right online communities and join the right conversations. Here are some examples of online communities:

- A LinkedIn group in which your target prospects participate

- A Twitter conversation (Tweet Chat) all about your service niche

- A conversation within the comments section of an influential niche blog

- A niche social network for your specific industry

Try to allocate resources to join these online groups and make relevant connections. If you are going to spend the time producing content, don't forget to promote it online.

"We've written tons of valuable content. So now what do we do?"

Bite sized is better

Which is more effective, one 20-page article or ten easy-to-skim blog posts? If you're resourceful, the answer can be both. Most professionals don't have enough time on their hands to produce a steady stream of content every month. That's why it makes sense to be thrifty with your content and find clever ways to have it do double duty.

The importance of a good offer cannot be underestimated.

The truth is that different audiences enjoy content in different formats. Some people skim blog posts in Google Reader while others like to print out entire eBooks and read them by the fire with a cup of cocoa. We do know that in the world of social media shorter is better. Catchy titles, bullet points, headers and videos spread more quickly than dense pages of text. Most web surfers don't have the time to read your manifesto over their lunch break.

Why not compromise? Write once and publish twice. Or more often! Here's how it works:

- Write a white paper

- Run a webinar on the same topic

- Take the main points of the webinar and write them up as a 3-part blog series

Here's another example:

- Write a seven-part blog series on a hot topic

- Then compile the posts into an educational guide that web visitors can download (don't forget to put it behind a registration form)

- Send out an e-newsletter that summarizes the guide and links to the download form

As you can see, there's no need to write every piece from scratch.

Getting your offers right

To many firms, the value of generating new website traffic is fairly clear — more visitors mean more opportunity, right? That's true, but only if you make it clear what visitors are supposed to do once they get to your site. Many websites don't feature any offers, so many of those opportunities go wasted.

> The truth is that different audiences enjoy content in different formats.

The importance of a good offer cannot be underestimated. After all, an offer is a means to a goal. So it pays to figure out how to get visitors to take an action. Then you need a way to measure these actions over time so that you can tinker with your offers and determine which ones perform best.

Offers come in two main flavors:

1. *Hard Offers* – For people late in the buying process, hard offers provide a straightforward way to contact your firm and inquire about your business.

   Example: "Ready to get started? Request a proposal."

2. Soft Offers – For folks who aren't ready to buy, soft offers keep the relationship going. Visitors exchange their name and email address for something they want (a guide or research report, for instance).

Example: "White Paper on Green Building Trends: 2012. Download Now"

If you strategically place offers throughout your firm's website, you can collect dozens of new leads each week. Then you can use email marketing to make additional soft offers and nurture the relationship. But be careful. The design and wording of your offers can have a dramatic effect on performance. And the offers must be relevant to your audience or they will ignore them. As you develop new offers, test them against the old versions. Over time you'll improve your conversion rate.

By now, you should have a pretty good understanding of this engine that drives online marketing. In the next chapter, we explore how you can keep the engine humming.

Key Takeaways

- Your website is the hub of your online marketing program.

- You need to create a variety of content to attract visitors to your site and entice them to become leads.

- Not all content needs to be new. Some of it can be repurposed to save you time and effort.

- Use social media to promote new content.

- Include hard and soft offers on your website to convert visitors into leads.

CASE STUDY
SEO for Accountants:
E. Cohen and Company

E. COHEN
AND COMPANY, CPAs

Building Profitable Ideas

In many respects, E. Cohen and Company, a CPA firm in Rockville, Maryland, is little different from other accounting firms. Except that they manage to generate approximately 40% of their firm's leads from the web. Director of Marketing, Richard Rawson, shared four key strategies any accounting firm should employ when taking on an online marketing campaign.

1. Find a Ring Leader

It's vital to designate one marketing person whose primary focus is the online world. All too often, firms don't give their website and online campaigns the priority they need to consistently generate leads.

In E. Cohen's case, Richard is that person. The firm invested in an expert that understands SEO and can focus on website performance.

2. Build an SEO Foundation

Richard decided to concentrate on geographic keywords, such as "Maryland CPAs." He then optimized specific pages of the firm's website for these terms, which attracted a new stream of high-quality visitors.

This initiative alone may be the most significant factor in E. Cohen's online success. By incorporating keywords that have relatively high search volume and that are not overly competitive, Richard was able to secure high Google rankings for important words and phrases.

Does SEO work for accountants? Absolutely. This firm is proof.

3. Nurture Leads Through Email Marketing
Every two weeks, E. Cohen sends out a newsletter that contains educational content. This strategy has helped the firm stay in front of prospective clients. Instead of sending promotional, self-serving emails, the firm offers helpful tips and news that keep readers engaged.

4. One Step at a Time
It's easy to become overwhelmed by the many online marketing strategies out there. From social media to SEO to content marketing, where is one to start?

Richard's approach is to focus on the tactics that produce results. Once one tactic begins to pay off (SEO for example), he spreads his focus to the next tactic (say, social media).

Instead of taking on the world in the first month, consider working your way into online marketing and tracking results as you go. This approach has worked for Richard and his team, and it has led to enhanced regional visibility and a consistent flow of online leads.

14

PUTTING IT ALL ★ TOGETHER

★

Forming the habits of success.

Y ou'll never get 40% of your business leads from your website by assigning an intern to place a few Google PPC ads and start a Twitter account. You have to integrate online marketing deeply into your business strategy.

If you want to achieve dramatic online results, you'll need to commit real resources to your website, search engine optimization, content marketing and other online tactics. That doesn't mean you have to drastically increase your overall marketing budget (remember, high growth firms achieve amazing results while spending *less* than average). But it will need to become part of your firm's DNA.

You'll never get 40% of your business leads from your website by assigning an intern to place a few Google PPC ads and start a Twitter account.

Shifting Your Business Agenda to Reflect a Digital Approach

How many resources you should allocate to online marketing will depend on several factors, including:

• Your industry

• Level of competition

• Online marketing experience (is your firm new to online marketing, or have you been working at it for awhile?)

• Your firm's goals and objectives

Some firms are able to accomplish their online goals online with half of one employee's time. Other firms hire teams of 4, 5, or 10 full-time employees to deliver their online marketing strategy (for example, an SEO specialist, a content editor, a social marketing strategist). And, as we described in Chapter 11, some firms decide to leave online marketing partly or entirely to outside experts.

If you choose to do some or all of the work in house, be clear up front how much time you will allocate to each role. Some of the them, especially writing and SEO, can be very time consuming. Committing to these resources, rather than making them a side job, will help your firm make an effective transition to online marketing.

It's a good idea to schedule weekly status meetings to review online marketing metrics with your team. Tracking and reporting on your progress are crucial to the long-term success of your program. As your marketing team works these meetings into their regular schedules, they will begin to make online marketing part of their professional lives.

Rhythm and consistency

Most online marketing tactics are implemented over the long term, so it's important to find a comfortable groove and stick with it. Decide what needs to be accomplished on a regular basis, and develop a rhythm for executing those tasks. Here are some examples of frequent tasks that you will want to incorporate into your firm's regular marketing activities:

KRISTOPHER B. JONES
Author, *Search Engine Optimization*

"To improve your rankings you must improve your authority in the eyes of search engines. Get involved in your respective online communities and don't be afraid to ask for links."

- Develop and maintain an editorial calendar that defines which content will be produced and promoted in the coming months

- Conduct keyword research monthly and regularly evaluate which pages on your website should be tweaked to push them higher in search results

- Publish one to three blog posts each week. When possible, incorporate keywords into the posts and promote them on social media

- Monitor your online brand with Google Alerts, join relevant industry conversations and make connections with influential bloggers

- Send an email once per week that promotes a webinar or offers valuable educational content

If you choose to do some or all of the work in house, be clear up front how much time you will allocate to each role.

TIM ASH

Author, *Landing Page Optimization*

"It is critical to measure the conversion rate for important actions on your website. For example, track the percentage of visitors on your site that fill out your contact form or download a white paper. Continually tweaking your website to improve conversion rates will likely result in more interaction and more leads."

Your firm's range of activities will vary depending on the strategy. Whatever tactics you choose to pursue, doing them consistently will build engagement and improve the chances of success.

Observe, Test and Refine

Online marketing is both an art and a science. So long as technology continues to evolve, so will online marketing tools and techniques. As a result, it's unwise to base your firm's strategy on research and book learning alone.

Instead, think of online marketing as a long-term, ongoing experiment. Firms that grow their business online are comfortable with change. If you get in the habit of testing and refining your approach, you will be successful.

- As mobile technologies get more sophisticated, the way we code websites will change. *Evolve and adjust.*

- When new social networks arise, the way people consume information will change. *Evolve and adjust.*

- Every time Google makes a change to its search algorithm, your web content may be penalized or promoted in the search results. *Evolve and adjust.*

If you embrace change, it doesn't matter what happens. If you discover that people coming to your website from Pinterest are downloading white papers and people from Facebook are not, you can adjust your strategy to focus on Pinterest. If keyword A is producing leads and keyword B is producing website exits, you can find more keywords like keyword A. Let the data guide your strategy, and then test that strategy until you find an approach that works for you.

Maintaining your online advantage over time

There's a common misconception that online marketing is about stealthy tricks and search engine manipulation. Do any of these tactics sound familiar to you?

- Having a web developer write a line of code on your website that mysteriously makes you rank higher in results

- Paying a social media company to increase your Twitter following by a thousand followers in one week

- Hiring a digital PR company to distribute your press release to 500 news outlets in a day

- Working with a guru who guarantees #1 Google rankings in under one month

If these claims sound unrealistic it's because they are. Even if these companies can deliver on their promises, you won't get the kind of long-term benefit that comes from doing things the right way. Successful online brands view their web presence as a long-term initiative. Don't spin your wheels looking for a loophole in the system that will generate short-term spikes in web traffic. Instead, spend your energy creating amazing content and making the most of today's technology to position your firm as a thought leader. A leader that any sane company would love to hire.

Key Takeaways

- If you don't give online marketing the resources and time to succeed, it's guaranteed to fail.

- Find a marketing rhythm that works for your firm. Then stick to it.

- Testing is the best way to get optimal results from online marketing.

- There are no online marketing shortcuts.

CASE STUDY
Fortinet: Social Media for Technology Services

F⊡RTINET.

It's easy to dismiss Facebook and Twitter as a waste of company time and a productivity killer. To be honest, sometimes they are. But in the case of Fortinet, an IT services firm with an extraordinary grasp of social media, there's nothing unproductive about them.

Marketing Senior Manager Maeve Naughton and her team have found unique ways to use popular social media tools to increase their brand visibility in the marketplace. "Social media is absolutely paying off. We can see our engagement numbers such as likes, followers and comments going up. We are more visible and our brand has become recognizable online."

Twitter
Who Runs It: Maeve, Senior Manager
Time Spent Per Day: 1 – 2 hours per day
Purpose: Customer support. Customers post issues and questions on Twitter and Fortinet responds with assistance. More and more people are Tweeting to get in touch with service providers, and Fortinet's presence shows they care.

Facebook
Who Runs It: Maeve, Senior Manager
Time Spent Per Day: 1 – 2 hours per day
Purpose: Relationship building. Maeve posts and responds to questions, engages with visitors in a friendly way, and builds trust.

LinkedIn
Who Runs It: HR Department and Maeve, Senior Manager
Time Spent Per Day: 1 hour per day
Purpose: Recruiting. Fortinet uses LinkedIn as a source for prospective employees. With an extensive Jobs section and high credibility, this social network is a prime place to discover talent. Fortinet also has a LinkedIn Group in which members can discuss network security issues.

YouTube
Who Runs It: Product Marketing Team
Time Spent Per Day: 1 – 2 hours per week
Purpose: Product demos. YouTube is the perfect place to house company videos. The product team takes advantage of this highly trafficked site by showcasing Fortinet's latest products and services.

Blog
Who Runs It: Technical Team
Time Spent Per Day: 1 – 2 hours per week
Purpose: Technical Education. Even the tech guys at Fortinet get involved in social media. Their blog focuses on threat research and highlights what's going on in their niche industry. This content positions them as thought leaders and also attracts web traffic.

CONCLUSION
Make way for the revolution.

An online marketing revolution is changing the marketplace forever. While traditional face-to-face marketing still works, it's no longer the best way to attract and nurture new business. And firms that don't adopt online marketing techniques soon are likely to be left behind as buyers increasingly turn to the convenience and power of the Internet to educate themselves and find the best qualified service providers. In fact, firms that join the revolution today are more likely to enjoy an early competitive advantage.

We wrote this book to help professional services marketers like you adapt to this new environment and begin making fundamental changes to your own marketing program. We've shown you which tools tend to get the best returns. And we've laid out a blueprint to get you started.

As you implement your own online marketing plan, we encourage you to return to this book again and again for helpful tips and insights. As you discover the joys and profits of online marketing, we'd love to hear about your experiences. Email us your stories at info@hingemarketing.com.

Good Luck, and don't forget to have fun along the way!

MEET
THE EXPERTS

To reflect best practices, we interviewed top experts in various online marketing disciplines.

We asked the experts a set of questions that correspond to our professional services survey.

In addition, we asked about their specific area of expertise and how it might be best applied to professional services firms.

The following experts participated in this research:

ANN HANDLEY
Chief Content Officer at Marketing Profs
Author, *Content Rules*
Twitter: @MarketingProfs

BRAD GEDDES
Founder of Certified Knowledge
Author, *Advanced Google Adwords*
Twitter: @bgtheory

BRYAN EISENBERG
Managing Partner at Eisenberg
Holdings, LLC
Author, *Waiting for Your Cat to Bark?*
Twitter: @TheGrok

DANNY DOVER
Senior SEO Manager at AT&T
Interactive
Author, *Search Engine Optimization
Secrets*
Twitter: @DannyDover

DAVID MEERMAN SCOTT
Marketing Strategist and Consultant
Author, *The New Rules of Marketing
and PR*
Twitter: @dmscott

ERIC ENGE
President at Stone Temple Consulting
Co-Author, *The Art of SEO*
Twitter: @stonetemple

GINNY REDISH
Founder of Redish & Associates Inc.
Author, *Letting Go of Words — Writing Web
Content that Works*
Twitter: @GinnyRedish

JAMES BESWICK
Founder of One Uproar
Author, *Ranking Number One*
Twitter: @oneuproar

JASON BURBY
Chief Analytics and Optimization
Officer at **ZAAZ**
Author, *Actionable Web Analytics*
Twitter: @JasonBurby

JENNIFER ABERNETHY
America's Social Business Stylist &
CEO, The Sales Lounge
Author, *The Complete Idiot's Guide to
Social Media Marketing*
Twitter: @SalesLounge

JIM BOYKIN
Founder & CEO of Internet Marketing
Ninjas (formerly We Build Pages)
Blog: www.internetmarketing ninjas.com/
blog/
Twitter: @jimboykin

JOE PULIZZI
Founder of the Content Marketing
Institute
Co-Author, *Get Content Get Customers*
and *Managing Content Marketing*
Twitter: @juntajoe

JUSTIN CUTRONI
Director of Intelligence at Cardinal Path
Author, *Google Analytics*
Twitter: @justincutroni

KRISTOPHER B. JONES
Founder / CEO, KBJ Capital
Author, *Search Engine Optimization*
Twitter: @krisjonescom

KRISTINA HALVORSON
Founder of Brain Traffic
Author, *Content Strategy for the Web*
Twitter: @halvorson

LON SAFKO
Social Media Strategist
Author, *The Social Media Bible*
Twitter: @longsafko

MARI SMITH
Social Media Consultant
Author, *The New Relationship Marketing*
Twitter: @MariSmith

MICHAEL FLEISCHNER
Founder, MarketingScoop.com
Author, *SEO Made Simple*
Twitter: @mfleischner

TIM ASH
CEO of SiteTuners & Founder of
Conversion Conference
Author, *Landing Page Optimization*
Twitter: @tim_ash

WILLIAM ALBERT
Director of the Design and Usability
Center at Bentley University
Author, *Measuring the User Experience*
Twitter: @UXMetrics

ABOUT
THE AUTHORS

LEE W. FREDERIKSEN, PH.D.

Lee is Managing Partner at Hinge, a premier professional services branding and marketing firm. He brings over 30 years of marketing experience to the firm's clients. Lee is a former tenured professor of psychology at Virginia Tech, author of numerous books and articles, and a successful entrepreneur. He's started and run three high-growth companies, including an $80 million runaway success. Lee has worked with many global brands, including American Express, Time Life, Capital One, Monster.com and Yahoo! He led the research studies that form the basis of the book. He is co-author of *Spiraling Up: How to Create a High Growth, High Value Professional Services Firm.*

lfrederiksen@hingemarketing.com
www.linkedin.com/in/leefrederiksen

SYLVIA MONTGOMERY, CPSM

As a seasoned marketing executive with origins in graphic design, Sylvia has led marketing teams at several technology and consulting firms—from start-ups to Fortune 500 firms. Sylvia is a published author and speaker; previously she has served as an adjunct professor at both Trinity College and the George Washington University. At Hinge, Sylvia is a senior partner and leads the firm's A/E/C practice, engaging with clients on a daily basis and driving Hinge's own marketing initiatives. Her on-the-ground experiences provide a "realistic" dimension to her practical advice. Sylvia is an active member of the Society for Marketing Professional Services (SMPS), DC Chapter.

smontgomery@hingemarketing.com
@BrandStrong
www.linkedin.com/in/sylviamontgomery

SEAN MCVEY

Sean is an experienced consultant with a background in digital marketing. He is an expert in improving online performance. Sean has a diverse skill set, including search engine optimization, social media strategy and website usability testing. Before joining Hinge, Sean worked as a marketing consultant, helping companies in the technology, publishing, healthcare and legal industries. He also worked several years as a consultant for Booz Allen Hamilton, where he specialized in business process analysis.

smcvey@hingemarketing.com
@seantmcvey
www.linkedin.com/in/seanmcvey

AARON TAYLOR

Aaron is a founding partner at Hinge. In his 20 years in the industry, he has been an award-winning designer, editor, strategist and writer. Over his career, he's conceived and implemented engaging brand strategies for many professional services firms. Aaron has been published widely in local, regional and national business publications and industry magazines. He is co-author of *Spiraling Up: How to Create a High Growth, High Value Professional Services Firm.*

ataylor@hingemarketing.com
www.linkedin.com/in/aarontaylorva

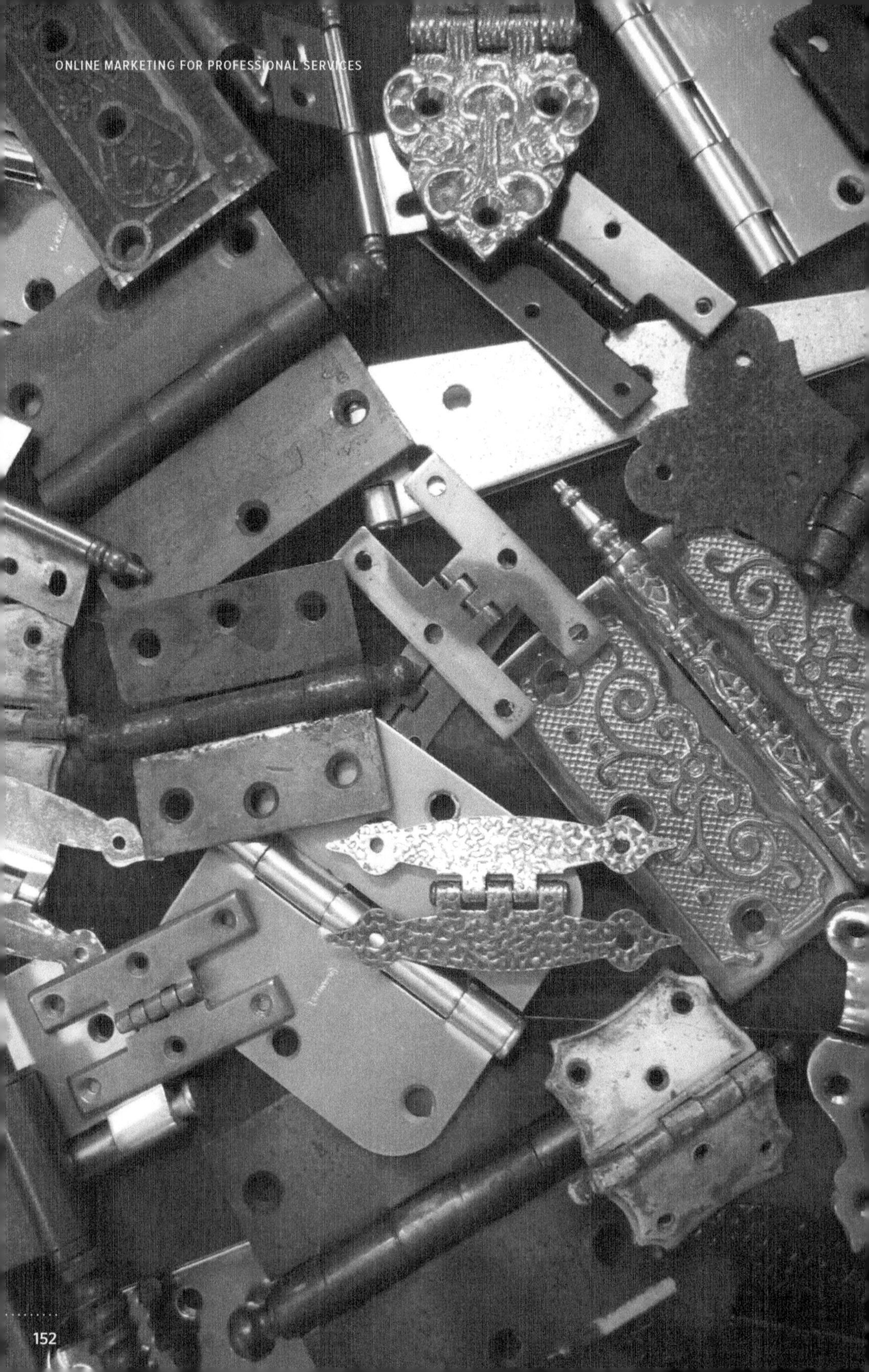

ABOUT HINGE

Hinge is a national branding and marketing firm that specializes in professional services. We conduct regular research into the industries that we serve — with a particular focus on high growth firms — so that we can offer professional services firms the insights and edge they need to break out in a marketplace that is undergoing fundamental change. We offer a comprehensive suite of online and offline marketing services that can help any firm build competitive advantage. To learn more, visit us at *www.hingemarketing.com*.

For free branding and marketing tips, advice and strategies for your professional services firm, follow us on Twitter and subscribe to our blog.

@HingeMarketing
www.hingemarketing.com/blog

About Hinge Research Institute

At Hinge, research is more than skin deep. It helps define who we are, how we help our clients and guides how we grow our firm. We believe in sharing our knowledge, not only with our clients but also with the broader professional services community. This commitment has led to the establishment of the Hinge Research Institute. The Institute is committed to conducting innovative research on professional services firms and their respective clients. We are also committed to sharing that knowledge through research studies, webinars, executive roundtables, whitepapers, articles and books. Please visit us at *www.hingeresearch.com* to find additional white papers, pod casts and research reports.

Resources

Spiraling Up: How to Create a High Growth, High Value Professional Services Firm
This book uncovers the secrets of high growth, high value professional services firms and describes what your firm can do to emulate them. *Free!*

Online Marketing for Professional Services Firms: How Digital Marketing Delivers Faster Growth and Higher Profits
In this groundbreaking study of 500 firms, you will learn how professional services marketing is undergoing profound change — away from traditional techniques and toward online marketing. *Free!*

Website Planning Guide: 7 Key Steps to Creating a High Performance, Lead-Generating Website
This guide will prepare you for one of the most important marketing investments your firm will make: the redesign and optimization of your firm's website. *Free!*

The Online Lead Generation Guide for Professional Services Firms
This insightful guide describes how lead generation is moving online and walks you through the steps to access a whole new world of qualified leads. *Free!*

Content Marketing Guide for Professional Services Firms
Find out how offering great content builds awareness and trust — and will revolutionize the way you sell professional services. *Free!*

The LinkedIn Guide for Professional Services Executives
Learn everything you need to know to get started with the most important social media platform for professional services executives. *Free!*

Professional Services Executives Forum
Join the only LinkedIn Group of professional services executives that explores how to build a high growth, high value professional services firm.

Professional Services Marketing Blog
Read the latest insights, real-world case studies and marketing tips from the minds of one of the nation's leading professional services marketing firms. Subscribe to the blog today. *www.hingemarketing.com/blog*